LOVE

THY

RIVAL

LOVE

THY

CHAD GIBBS

Blue Moon Books

NEW YORK LONDON PARIS GLENCOE

Blue Moon Books

Love Thy Rival
Copyright © 2012 by Chad Gibbs

This title is available as an eBook. Visit www.chadgibbs.com/lovethyrival

This title is not available in an audio edition, however for $22 dollars an hour the author will come to your house and read the book aloud. Warning: The author reads slowly, and he types words better than he pronounces them.

Este título no está disponible en Español.

Gibbs, Chad
Love Thy Rival: What sports' greatest rivalries teach us about loving our enemies
ISBN 978-0985716509 (softcover)

Note: Some of the names in this book have been changed to protect the innocent. Others were changed to protect the guilty. Other were possibly misspelled. Statistics and all-time records cited in this book will quickly become out of date. There is no need for you to email me about this. Blue Moon Books is an imaginary publishing house, created to hide the fact that this book was self-published. There is no need for you to email me about this either.

Editor: Shelby D. Zacharias
Copy Editor: Anne Hoekman
Cover and Interior Design: Brian Brown
Favorite Beatles Album: Sgt. Pepper's Lonely Hearts Club Band

4   8   15   16   23   42

For that little red-haired girl

Contents

But I say unto you, Love your enemies

- Matthew 5:44

A Time to Hate

Prologue

Last Christmas, after opening presents, but before the turkey-induced nap, my in-laws and I discussed my plans for a second book.

"In a way," I told them, "my first book was a love story."

They nodded, their faces revealing concern for their youngest daughter, who had apparently married a man who considers books about football romantic.

"What I mean," I clarified, "is that I wrote about how we identify with our teams, in almost the same way we identify with our church or our family. We love our teams, often times more than we should, and the book looked at the problems that can cause."

My mother-in-law, who was still angry her scene from my first book was cut by the editor, asked, "So what's this new book going to be about?"

"I want to write a book on rivalries, and not just in college football, but the most intense rivalries in all of sports. I want to look at how fans in these rivalries interact, and more importantly, I want to examine the role of hate in sports."

At that moment, my niece Ava, who is wise beyond her three years, gasped and said, "Uncle Chad, we're not supposed to say hate."

The rest of the family smiled, then mockingly scolded me for using the four letter word.

"That's right," I said. "I forgot. We're not supposed to say hate."

But we do.

Auburn vs. Alabama

Bryant-Denny Stadium – Tuscaloosa, Alabama
November 26, 2010

If a man say, I love God, and hateth his brother, he is a liar.
—1 John 4:20

It was 2:30 a.m. when I finally looked at the clock to know the full measure of my shame. I couldn't believe it. I had gone to bed four and a half hours ago, exhausted, but now felt as if some demented nurse was giving me Red Bull intravenously. I shut my eyes again. The dread was still there though, the dread that began with this simple thought: "If we win the toss tomorrow, I wonder if we'll kick or receive."

That question was all it took to flood my mind with nightmare scenarios, all ending with an Auburn loss to Alabama and, for some reason, me being thrown off the top of the upper deck. I gave up and turned on the television. ESPN was replaying a panel of talking heads breaking down tomorrow's, make that today's game. Three of them thought Auburn would win, while one was convinced we would lose, and for some reason I decided that man had the most important opinion on earth. As the dread increased, I turned off the television and tried to sleep, tossing and turning for hours. Eventually I counted sheep, but even this proved harrowing, as the eighth one mutated into Alabama receiver Julio Jones, who sprouted wings, making him virtually impossible to cover man to man. Okay, I may have fallen asleep at this point, but even the two and a half hours I did sleep were not restful.

I had a book signing that morning in Tuscaloosa before the game. My first book, *God and Football*, had released three months earlier. I'd spent most Saturdays that fall sitting at tables in campus bookstores watching people pick up my book, look at me, put down my book, and walk away. This morning figured to be no different, but I dressed in neutral colors anyway, as to not offend fans on either side.

Everyone who walked past my table looked at least as nervous as I was, and I don't think anyone really considers buying books when they are anxious. In the end, I signed only nine, a third of those to friends, and afterward I walked from the Ferguson Center to Bryant-Denny Stadium in a cold drizzle.

Kickoff was ninety minutes away, but people were already entering the stadium. I checked the gate number on my soggy ticket and walked inside. My seat was in the north end zone, the visitor's section, and I walked in an upward spiral for what seemed like hours until I finally reached the top. It was there, in the upper levels of the jet stream, that I realized how woefully underdressed I was. I left my seat, briefly pondered the ramifications of buying an Alabama sweatshirt from the souvenir booth, then sat for thirty minutes in a bathroom stall to avoid the wind and rain.

Closer to kickoff I ventured back out into the elements and sat down next to my friend Chris Harrison,[1] who appeared to be wearing every article of clothing he owned. He might actually survive a fall from the upper deck if we were both tossed over, but I decided not to mention this particular fear to him.

Soon the Million Dollar Band was on the field, we sang our national anthem, and then the captains called the coin toss—the coin toss that kept me up most of the night. Auburn won, and they kicked the ball. Chris and I both thought this a little strange,

---

1. The pharmacist, not the host of *The Bachelor.* Shut up, my wife makes me watch it.

considering our Tigers had Cam Newton and the most explosive offense in school history, but we figured the coaches probably knew what they were doing. It was 7–0, Alabama, before we could sit down.

I turned to Chris, who looked like he'd seen Bear Bryant's ghost. I probably looked worse but tried to keep my cool. "We just need to match that score and then the team will settle down." Chris agreed, but the Tigers promptly went three and out. One punt later, Greg McElroy threw to a wide-open Julio Jones. It was 14–0, Alabama.

"Okay," Chris said. "We just need to take the ball, drive down, and score, and we're right back in it. It's still very early." I agreed. But Auburn went three and out again. McElroy to Hanks. 21–0, Bama.

I looked at the clock, then at the scoreboard, and began making calculations. "If we go down 28–0, I'm leaving."

Another three and out for Auburn, and I reached for my keys as Alabama's Mark Ingram ran toward the goal line. It's strange, but my memory of a big play I see in person is usually replaced by the television replay that I will inevitably rewatch hundreds of times. Except I still see this play the way I saw it from my seat: Antoine Carter hitting Ingram from behind at about the twenty-yard line, punching the ball loose, the ball then tight-roping the sideline all the way to the back of the end zone. Touchback.

I high-fived Chris and laughed. I didn't think Auburn would win the game, I wasn't even sure we'd score, but it was the first thing that had gone right all day. The Tigers of course gave the ball right back, and in the twinkling of an eye Alabama was knocking on the goal line again. But this time Auburn's defense held, to a degree, forcing a field goal. 24–0. "That's really only three scores," Chris said.

"I know," I said. "Think how bad it would be if Julio had wings."

Just then my phone buzzed in my pocket. It was a seven-word

text from my wife, Tricia, who was stuck at work and had just seen the score.

It read, "Just get the #$%@ out of there."

~~~

It had already been an interesting fall, even before Greg McElroy's 300-yard first half sent my wife into a cursing text rage. My book, which chronicled my struggle to balance faith in God with passion for pigskin, released just days before the season began. In the book, I didn't uncover a ten-step plan to help other fans—I don't think there are one-size-fits-all solutions to these types of problems—I just came to the realization that football is a great hobby, but a terrible god. And when I look to football, or anything apart from God, for my self worth and identity, then I'm in dangerous waters.

The book wasn't groundbreaking, but it was very relatable. I heard from fans all over the South who struggle just like me. Some found a healthier balance through the years, while others were still searching. Going into the 2010 season, I was ready for that first loss. I would face it with my newfound spiritual maturity and prove to the world, and myself, that football no longer held dominion over my life. I count it pure coincidence that as soon as I began selling my book, the Auburn football team forgot how to lose.

Early wins against South Carolina and Clemson filled us with hope, as did a last-second comeback in a revenge game against Kentucky. Then came Arkansas, a team that for some reason has given Auburn fits through the years, so much so that I willingly scheduled a book signing in Gainesville, Florida, for the day of the game. At that signing I had the following conversation with a Gator lady. "Well," she asked, somewhat mockingly, "Are you better after you wrote this book? Can your team lose and you still find the strength to go to church the next morning?"

I laughed and said, "Beats me, Auburn hasn't lost since I wrote the book."

She didn't laugh, but said, "Maybe God is just setting you up for a big test at the end of the season."

I replied the only way I could: "Get behind me, Satan."

It's hard not to think that life is just a movie about you, and all your friends and family are the supporting cast, while those nameless people you cross paths with are extras. It's even harder when you write a book about football, then start getting daily emails from people wanting to know how the current season is affecting you.

Sure, I believed that lady when she said Auburn was probably going to lose a game, but I didn't think God was orchestrating this undefeated run just to provide me with a spiritual test. But now that Auburn was 11–0, three wins away from a national title, and trailing our archrival by twenty-four points, I began to think maybe she was right.

The Bama game was the fourth time that season that Auburn trailed by double digits, but it was the first time I felt like vomiting. Until that point in the season, I had achieved a level of blissful detachment. I could celebrate victories like I played a part in the win, and, if they came, I would shrug off defeats like they were no more than a mild nuisance in my otherwise wonderful day. But here I was, making myself sick once again, over a stupid game.

Sports are exciting. Sometimes it's hard to sleep the night before a big game, the same way it's hard for kids to sleep the night before Christmas. I don't think there is anything wrong with this. But with rivalry games, there is no excitement, only dread. I wasn't wide awake at 2:30 a.m. before the Iron Bowl thinking about how awesome it was going to be when Auburn beat Alabama. I could only picture losing, followed by the 365 days of ridicule that would surely follow.

I wonder if this has something to do with hate.

~~~

Hate is a strong word, but it is a word I use often in conversation. A friend with a different, perhaps better outlook on life told me, "I only use the H-word when talking about specific foods." I, on the other hand, hear myself saying it all the time. Just the other day I saw Kim Kardashian on television and said out loud, "I hate her."

Seriously? I don't even know her. I don't know anyone who knows her. Yet I decided she deserves my utmost contempt, simply because she happened to be on *Entertainment Tonight*. I should hate myself for watching that show to begin with.

Faced with this realization, I did what I always do when something bothers me: I found someone smarter to talk to. I called Al Jackson, pastor of Lakeview Baptist Church in Auburn, where I attended during college.

We sat in his office, and I explained my problem. "When I say I hate another team or their coach or their fans, I feel like most of the time it's a joke, it's just something I say. And when I go to a game and spew out this stuff, I know it's not real, but it has to affect me, right? I mean, I can't go to a game and produce this sort of bile for four hours and not be changed for the worse."

"Yes, it affects us," Brother Al said, and as we spoke about rivalries, he told me a story from the 1974 Iron Bowl. "I was in seminary in Fort Worth, and Kem and I came home for Thanksgiving. We spent Thursday with our families, and on Friday we drove to Birmingham for the game. Auburn lost 17–13. We had a touchdown called back late; Thomas Gossom caught a ball and was called out of bounds. I thought it was a controversial call, but nevertheless we lost. And over the next several weeks, I experienced all the classic stages you go through when a loved one dies. I had denial. I had anger. I had grief."

"And all that," I asked, "the denial and anger, it wasn't because we lost to just anyone, but because we lost to Bama?"

"Of course. And you know what, the Holy Spirit jumped all over me. He said, 'You are way out of bounds, this is wrong,' so

I humbled myself before God best I knew how, and I repented before God. I begged God to deliver me from all of that, and He did, and I've been free from it for thirty-six years. When you find sports doing this to you, you've got to step back and ask yourself, 'How is this honoring God?'"

~~~

That's been my fear all along, that my passion for sports is not honoring God. Not only that, but I'm starting to fear some of my lower moments, usually brought on by the Auburn–Alabama rivalry, may actually be dishonoring God. I've read what Jesus says about loving your enemies, and I have trouble loving people who cheer for a different football team than I do. If I can't love rival fans, how will I ever be able to love my actual enemies, people who would want to harm me for my faith? If sports are a test, I'm failing miserably.

I conducted a survey while writing this book, asking people if they talk differently about rival fans when those fans are not around. Most do. I know I do. I'll catch myself saying things about Bama fans that I would never say in front of my friends who cheer for Alabama, or my dear mother, who bleeds crimson. Maybe it's not hate, but it's not good. It's generalizing, and it's stereotyping, and it's sort of the way racists think.

I understand that this sports hate isn't the biggest problem facing our world today. No genocidal maniac is going to try to rid the world of Yankees fans. But when sports keep us from being the people we're called to be, it's a problem. I fear that fans cheering for teams in these great rivalries have a tougher course to navigate.

I was thinking about this after Auburn's historic comeback in the Iron Bowl. The Tigers cut the lead to 24–7 at the half and scored on the second play of the third quarter to make it 24–14. A Cam Newton run brought the score to 24–21, and then a fourth quarter touchdown catch by Philip Lutzenkirchen finally gave Auburn the 28–27 lead they did not relinquish. In the somewhat surreal celebration that followed, Auburn fans, myself included, sang our version of "Rammer Jammer," in which we invite Tide fans to go where "their worm dieth not, and the fire is not quenched."[2] Outside the stadium I saw friends, and the looks on their faces were not those of fans whose team had just won, but of patients who'd just been told their tumors were benign. We all sensed the relief and hugged each other the way people hug when world wars come to an end.

After the Iron Bowl, I received an email from a man living south of Birmingham, and he told me how his Sunday school class had nearly broken up over it. It seems members of the class had waged electronic war against each other after the game on Facebook. The Sunday after the game, a tearful class leader begged God during the closing prayer to help the class once again find unity.

I shook my head and began to wonder aloud why this game in particular brings out such different emotions, why rivalry games are different. Tricia stopped me and said with a deep sigh, "You're going to write another book, aren't you?"

"I'm thinking about it," I said. "I felt like I answered so many of my questions with the first book, only to get hammered with a new set of questions this year."

"And I guess you're going to want to do all sports now, not just SEC football, so you'll be flying all over the place, buying expensive tickets, and living the dream life while I stay in Auburn and doctor sick children."

"You can go with me on some of the trips."

"Oh, thanks."

"I'll dedicate the book to you."

"Right, that's every girl's dream isn't it, to have their husbands dedicate a book about hate to them."

We sat in silence. I could tell she hated me, but I couldn't tell if it was real hate, or just writer-wife hate, so I did the only thing

2. Hell, for those of you not familiar with Mark 9:48

I could. I begged.

"Can I do it, please, please, please?"

"Oh, all right."

With blessing in hand, I set out to explore the most heated rivalries in sports. I knew early on I wouldn't be able to see every great rivalry, and a couple of the ones I did see may seem obscure, but I did cover all of the major sports, along with a few minor ones. I saw rivalries in which the teams share a zip code, and others that are cross-country. Some are older than the leagues that govern them, while others are younger than I am. Some of these games are played once a year; others happen nearly twenty times a season. Each rivalry is unique, but they all have one thing in common: their fans, well, they just don't like each other.

What follows is what happened as best as I can remember. I harbor no pretensions that a book like this can change the world. I just want you to laugh and buy everyone you know a copy for Christmas. If by the end we learn that this hate, or whatever it is that makes rivalry games different, can teach us something about loving our enemies, then maybe we can find a way to do some good.

Kentucky vs. Louisville

KFC Yum! Center – Louisville, Kentucky
December 31, 2010

To really know someone is to have loved and hated him in turn.
—Marcel Jouhandeau

I love my job.

I was sprawled across my bed at the Hyatt Regency Louisville when this occupational affection crossed my mind. It was a few minutes after seven, and after the eight-hour drive from Auburn, I tried to relax before my growling stomach drove me back out into the cold to search for nourishment. The sound of horse hooves hitting pavement drew me to the window, and I wondered aloud who would take a Thursday evening carriage ride through downtown Louisville. After four or five carriages passed, I realized the answer was everyone except me. Glancing up, I noticed the office building across Fourth Street. Almost every window was lit with a fluorescent glow, and almost every desk was still occupied by some weary soul. I watched them work, fidget, and yawn, then I glanced at my clock and shook my head, thanking God that I was in my window and not theirs.

Dinner came courtesy of Qdoba, a Mexican restaurant that apparently doesn't understand the proper use of the letter Q. I walked outside and noticed a Borders bookstore across the street. Checking to see if a bookstore has copies of my first book, *God and Football*, has proved to be an irresistible temptation, and without Tricia there to make fun of me, I strolled in. They had two copies, which pleased me greatly, and I discreetly moved them to the shelf with employee recommendations, right next to *Twilight*, where they belong. Then, fighting the temptation of a solitary carriage ride through the Derby City, I retired to my room and watched the end of the Music City Bowl. Just before sleep and I found each other, a knock on my door startled me.

"Hello?" I said, more of a question than a greeting.

"Who is this?" asked the voice on the other side.

"That's not how this works," I replied.

I could hear multiple voices outside, and looking through the keyhole, I saw six or seven teenagers.

"We're looking for this guy," one of them said.

"I think his name is Steve," said another.

"Yeah, we are looking for Steve," said the first voice. "He owes us $600, and he said he'd be staying in this hotel."

"Well, my name is Chad," I said, "and I don't owe any of you money, so I'm going back to bed."

"Wait, I think his name was Chad," said one of the girls in the group.

I flung open the door, and they all jumped backward. Seeing that I was not, in fact, Steve, they began to apologize profusely.

"Sorry, man, you're not the guy we are looking for."

"Yeah, sorry man."

With that they walked away, and I heard them knocking on my neighbor's door, asking for Steve, or someone, who owed them $600. So I picked up the phone and called the front desk to have them killed or thrown out or whatever it is nice hotels do to these types. Then I went to sleep. I had a long day of work ahead of me, and by work I mean watching Louisville and Kentucky play basketball.

I love my job.

~~~

I didn't know much about the Kentucky–Louisville rivalry going into this trip. I checked Amazon for a book on the background, but that book didn't exist. So I went to Wikipedia and noticed the teams didn't start playing regularly until 1983. I thought, "I'm six years older than this rivalry, how intense could it possibly be?"

Then I talked to the fans.

"I would rather my daughter be a whore than a Democrat or a Louisville fan."

Rob, a Wildcats fan from Prospect, Kentucky, sent me that gem in an email, with what I pray is a touch of hyperbole.

"If you see me with a towel on my head, it means Kentucky is playing Al Qaeda."

That came from Lance, a Louisville fan from southern Indiana, although even he admits there is no way Al Qaeda could handle Kentucky's press.

There's more than a little animosity bubbling under the surface here, but why? Both schools are in Kentucky, and the campuses are fewer than eighty miles apart, so the fans can't be that different, can they?

"Not to stereotype," said Tracy from Owensboro, when speaking of Louisville fans, "but their irrational ignorance carries over into other aspects of life, which makes them essentially intolerable."

"We tend to be the more intelligent of the two," said UofL fan John Adams. "They are the dumbest, slowest progressing people in this country. You can see many examples of this on YouTube."[1]

After talking to dozens of partisans from each school, I got the impression that all Louisville fans smoke menthols, grow line beards, and own multiple flat-billed hats. While all Kentucky fans wear overalls and drive tractors to their Klan meetings.

I tried to dig deeper, to see if this animosity concerned fans. Asking, in light of their faith, whether they worried this rivalry

---

1. I tried to verify this on YouTube, but I only found cats playing keyboards.

might be unhealthy.

"I'm an atheist," said Lewis Sanders. "UK basketball is my religion, and Rupp Arena is my church. If I were to reexamine my hate for Louisville, it would be much like a Baptist reevaluating their hate of Satan."

Fair enough, but even when I asked fans with religious beliefs, many gave the same answer.

"It's not real hate. It's pretend hate, sports hate, just for fun."

So you wouldn't have any trouble marrying a fan of the other school, right?

"Never," said Tyler Vincent. "I would rather go through life a virgin than marry a Louisville fan."

Tyler wasn't the only one with this view of matrimony. Many Louisville fans told me they wouldn't give Ashley Judd the time of day. Then I heard from fans who left their churches because the preacher was a fan of their rival school. This may not be genocidal hate, but it's certainly more than just pretend.

Drew Deener, host of The Early Birds on WKRD 790AM in Louisville, confirmed this when we spoke a few weeks after the game. Drew, once a familiar voice to Kentucky fans, now works for the Cardinals.

"I'd pretty much ridden the fence until this year," Drew told me. "But I finally went on air and said, you know what, the emails about my family have become too personal, so I'm out on Kentucky."

Drew's conversion cost him his Twitter account, which was flooded with some shockingly vulgar farewells from his Kentucky followers.

"In this business you expect the occasional 'screw you,' it goes with the territory. But you don't expect people wishing ill will on your family."

While people change jobs all the time, only a few know the joy, and by joy I mean torture, of moving from one rival to another. Former Kentucky and current Louisville head coach

Rick Pitino is one of the few. Nearly half the emails I received from UK and UofL fans mentioned Pitino. Many admit his move to Louisville escalated the animosity of this rivalry to unprecedented levels. Chris Hahn, Lead Executive Pastor of Southland Christian Church in Lexington, told me, "I wouldn't categorize most of the ribbing between Kentucky and Louisville fans as hate, but there is definitely a level of hatred there, especially after Pitino went to Louisville. There was genuine hatred toward him from UK fans."

Genuine hatred because a man changed jobs. But it wasn't just any job change. Fans understand coaches don't stay at a school for forty years these days. When Pitino left Kentucky for the Boston Celtics, the Big Blue Nation was grateful for the program he built in Lexington and wished him well. Many became Celtics fans. But when Pitino joined Louisville in 2001, UK fans viewed it as a slap in the face, while UofL fans welcomed their former tormentor with open arms.

This is the problem we fans have. We identify so strongly with our teams, they become such a part of who we are, that decisions having nothing to do with us are seen as slaps in the face. Some of you will think hating someone because they left your basketball team to coach another is the stupidest thing you've ever heard. In more rational moments, I think it's stupid too. But oh, do I get it.

~~~

The next morning, after a breakfast of champions, waffles and a Diet Coke, I walked from the hotel to the KFC Yum! Center, perhaps the only arena in the country with an exclamation point in its name. The KFC Yum! Center (which unfortunately doesn't have a shorter nickname I can substitute)[2] opened in October 2010 and was built for an estimated $238 million. For the previous fifty-four seasons, Louisville played its home games at Freedom Hall, another multi-purpose arena just south of down-

---

2. How about 'The House that Clogged Arteries Built'.

town, closer to the UofL campus.

Perched on the banks of the Ohio River, the KFC Yum! Center is a spectacular, state-of-the-art building. I sat outside next to a fountain and watched Kentucky and Louisville fans pass by. I hoped someone would start a fistfight in my vicinity. That may sound farfetched, but this is Kentucky, home of the Hatfields and McCoys[3] , so you never know.

No one seemed interested in violence, so I went inside early to check out the new arena. Upon walking through the doors, I found myself at the end of a line of likeminded people. Word from the front was we would be allowed inside in twenty minutes, so I eavesdropped on the conversations around me.

"Your new arena is beautiful," said a woman in blue to a man in red next to her.

"Oh, thank you, we are very proud of it," replied the man with a smile.

Excuse me? Don't you people hate each other? If your rival builds a new arena, aren't you supposed to say stuff like, "You paid $238 million for this dump? I hope I'm not inside when it crumbles to the ground and buries you all alive." But all around me similar, frustratingly civil conversations were taking place. I couldn't help but think of the old Warner Bros. cartoon where the wolf and sheepdog spend all day trying to kill each other, only to stop at the sound of a whistle, then proceed to clock out for the day, walking off to enjoy each other's company at dinner. Perhaps these schools subscribe to the time clock concept of hate. Or maybe it was too early in the morning.

After twenty amicable minutes, we were let in to roam the KFC Yum! Center. The place is amazing, and as you would expect, full of Taco Bells, KFCs, and Pizza Huts. Something I didn't expect was the bars. Not just beer, mind you. Although it seems foreign to someone who mostly attends games in the

3. The Hatfields and McCoys fought for over thirty years on the Kentucky-West Virginia border. Their feud, which like all great feuds began over a pig, claimed the lives of at least twelve people.

teetotaling Southeastern Conference, the KFC Yum! Center has full service bars. I chomped on a late morning taco and watched students line up for Bloody Marys. Maybe now the hate would start to flow.

After the taco and a ten-minute lesson from a chatty tablemate on the difference between a state and a commonwealth, I headed to my seat, which was—arghhh—in the stupid student section. I'm not saying the students were stupid; I just wasn't excited about sitting in the student section because (a) I'm thirty-three years old, and (b) I wasn't wearing a bucket of chicken on my head.

I know that last point doesn't make much sense, but there were dozens of girls wearing old KFC buckets on their heads. Many had cut holes on each side for their pigtails to stick out. I expect to see this look on the runways of Milan's next fashion week.

But the main reason I didn't want to sit in the student section was because I know how they work. If it were general admission, it would have been okay, because I could have found a seat near the top and minded my own business. But the Louisville student section has assigned seats, and when that's the case, only half of the students seem to care.

I was sitting in my original seat, right behind the goal and about fifteen rows up, when a guy and two girls came and stood beside me. "Hey man, if you are by yourself, would you mind sitting in my original seat so the three of us can sit together?"

The game of musical chairs began. Next came five shirtless guys with letters painted on their chests, and they needed my seat to spell out CARDS instead of ARDS, so I moved again.

Finally I found myself in a row with three empty seats to my left and four to my right. Tip-off was five minutes away, and I began to fantasize about watching the game with two elbow rests.

"These are our seats."

I looked up and saw a gaggle of attractive sorority girls.

"I have Seat 15," I said, holding up my ticket stub.

The lead girl was unmoved by this visual proof and repeated herself. "These are our seats."

"Okay, I'll move," I said. It wasn't worth spending the entire game sitting among seven angry girls, but I wanted someone to admit that #15 was, indeed, my seat. "But this is technically my seat."

"These are our seats," said the girl, this time with a snarl.

I shuffled past the girls toward the aisle, hating them more with each step. But weeks later my anger has waned, and I realize it would be a gross misuse of my position to mention that these girls belonged to the Kappa Delta sorority, so I won't.

Walking back up the aisle, I scanned the rows for single seats, only to meet the glaring eyes of angry students who, like the kids on Forrest Gump's bus, said, "Seat's taken." I reached the top of the lower level, where a standing room only bar overlooks the arena. There I found a spot at the end of the bar and settled in for a game on my feet.

~~~

This year's game promised to be a good one, with both teams ranked in the Top 20, but the fact that it was even taking place is a story in itself. By 1983 the rivalry lay dormant for close to sixty years, with only the occasional NCAA tournament game bringing the teams together. For over a decade, Louisville coach Denny Crum lobbied for the two natural rivals to play annually, but UK coach Joe B. Hall would not budge from former coach Adolph Rupp's longstanding policy not to play other Kentucky schools.

I'm sure Louisville fans relished in teasing their Kentucky friends that the Wildcats were scared of the Cards, but that doesn't appear to have been the case. "They didn't want to give us any inroads in terms of recruiting," said Crum. "They had the advantage throughout the state, and they wanted to maintain that advantage." Seems Kentucky didn't want to play Louisville because they didn't want to legitimize Louisville, but after four Final Fours and a national championship, Crum legitimized the Cardinals on his own. Fate brought the two together in the 1983 regional final, a game fans called the Dream Game.

A great YouTube video details the buildup to the Dream Game, including an awesomely awkward interview between Joe B. Hall and, of all people, John Tesh. The Cardinals won the game in overtime and afterward no one, including Governor John Y. Brown Jr., was going to let the rivalry lay dormant any longer. In November 1983, the series resumed and has been played every year since.

~~~

The most recent renewal of the Kentucky–Louisville rivalry had included fifty-one fouls, five of those technicals, and on more than one occasion players had to be separated before punches were thrown. I hoped for a repeat this morning, although it would be great if the fights were not broken up and occasionally spilled into the crowd. Much to my chagrin, the closest thing I saw to a fight was between me and a sorority. The game, however, was intense.

Louisville's Preston Knowles buried a three to start the scoring. I thought the capacity crowd would bring their new arena crumbling to the ground. Moments later when Kyle Kuric made another three for Louisville, I almost ran for safety. But the Cats hung tough, eventually taking the lead, 15–14. By halftime that lead grew to 35–24.

All around me people looked sick, even some of the Kentucky fans. I'm not sure what, but there's just something about these games. There isn't joy in victory, but relief. I thought of Lance Taubman, a Kentucky fan I'd spoken to before the game, who told me, "It isn't even fun to play them anymore. I'm a nervous wreck."

The second half was all Josh Harrellson. The six foot, ten inch Kentucky senior scored eighteen of his twenty-three points to go along with his fourteen rebounds in the half. Louisville fought hard and cut into the Wildcat lead during the second half, one time slashing it to ten. However the ball always wound up in Harrellson's hands, where he proceeded to dunk it, delighting those in Blue and infuriating the Cardinal masses, including the two men beside me who kept yelling, "Stupid cracker!" Harrellson is white. So were the men beside me. I think it says a lot when you hate your rival so much you use racial slurs on your own race.

Kentucky pulled away late, winning 78–63. By the end, Kentucky fans were a loud minority in the KFC Yum! Center, singing and cheering their victorious Wildcats. This is generally a great time for altercation spotting, but Louisville fans seemed content to let the Big Blue Nation enjoy their win. It was New Year's Eve, so everyone had something to look forward to that evening.

~~~

After my trip, I talked to Dave Stone, senior pastor of Southeast Christian Church in Louisville. Dave has been a Cardinals fan for thirty years, and his church has a weekly attendance that would fill up the KFC Yum! Center.[4]

The fans who told me they would leave a church if the pastor was an outspoken fan of their rival must not attend Southeast. Dave told me, "There's probably not a month that goes by during basketball or football season that I don't make a snide remark toward UK." Dave admits there is a limit to these jokes. "I've found a glancing blow is acceptable, but people can get pretty irate if it's anything more than that."

I asked Dave about hate in the rivalry, and he said, "I don't think it goes as far as hate with the masses. There are a lot of people who can turn it off when the game is over. I think *hate* is a pretty strong word, and when it's all said and done, 95 percent of the fans understand it's just a game."

---

4. In fact, Dave told me that when Southeast was being built, people driving by thought it was going to be a massive basketball arena, until they stuck a giant cross on top.

From Dave's observations, alcohol tends to fuel the problem. "A person who is just a nominal jerk can put it on afterburners when alcohol is in the mix."

Finally, I asked what leads some fans to take rivalries too far, and Dave said, "Usually it's people that don't have a whole lot to live for. So they get wrapped up in living only for this world, and they look for something to fill the void."

I tend to agree with Dave that 95 percent of fans understand it is just a game. Problem is, the KFC Yum! Center and Rupp Arena both hold over twenty thousand fans. So at each game you've got over a thousand people who don't realize it's just a game. These are the people I worry about, because sometimes I'm among their number.

~~~

Crossing the Ohio River, I left Louisville and for the first time in my life entered Indiana. Judging from my one stop, Indiana is a friendly state with clean restrooms. Driving the length of the state, however, is not the most exhilarating way to spend an afternoon. It's sort of like watching a six-hour-long John Cougar Mellencamp video.

I spent the night in Hammond, Indiana. I'd wanted to stay in Chicago, but it was New Year's Eve and hotel prices were outrageous. I found this place, which was a couple of stars lower than my Louisville hotel.

"I need to see your credit card for incidentals, and you must sign this waiver saying you will not throw a party in your room tonight."

I reached for my wallet, then, finally taking in what I'd just heard, said to the desk clerk, "There isn't a possible scenario that ends with me throwing a party in my hotel room tonight."

"Just sign here, please."

I took off my shoes, sat on the bed, and took a deep breath. It was finally dawning on me that I was about to spend New Year's Eve in a 2-star hotel in Hammond, Indiana, alone. I called Tricia.

She'd had a long day at work, and we both complained about how tired we were, and how staying up until midnight didn't seem like an option.

"I think I'll just watch Seacrest ring in the Eastern Time Zone and go to bed," Tricia said.

"I'm in the Eastern Time Zone, so technically I'll get to see it."

"Well, good for you," Tricia said, with a bit of snark.

I bit my tongue because I know Tricia suffers from Harry-Sally Syndrome. This rare disorder causes her to expect every New Year's Eve to be just like the final scene of *When Harry Met Sally*. When the evening inevitably lets her down, she spirals into a twenty-four-hour funk.

Trying to cheer her up, I recalled something I'd just read about the Hatfields and McCoys. "You know, it could be worse. One hundred and twenty-three years ago tonight, all the Hatfields had to do on New Year's Eve was sit around and organize a massacre."

Tricia was quiet for a second, then said, "Well, at least they had *something* to do."

With that we said good night. An hour later Ryan Seacrest counted down from ten, the earth completed its giant lap around the sun, and I went to bed. Exactly one hour later, as I dreamed of being chased by Kappa Deltas with KFC buckets on their heads, the sky outside my hotel window exploded into multicolored chaos. It was midnight. Apparently Hammond, Indiana, is on Central Time, and I had missed New Year's for the first time I could remember.

I hate my job.

Bears vs. Packers

Lambeau Field – Green Bay, Wisconsin
January 2, 2011

All men kill the thing they hate, too, unless, of course, it kills them first.
—James Thurber

It's fifteen degrees and a Bears fan walks past my car wearing only a T-shirt. This alone could be used as evidence to send him to an asylum for life, not to mention the fact that we are in Green Bay and his T-shirt reads, "Jesus Hates the Packers." And to think I almost missed this. I'd intended to cover the Dallas–Washington rivalry for the NFL chapter. In my mind, that was *the* NFL rivalry. Numerous Top 10 lists around the Internet agreed, and besides, it's cowboys and Indians, the only rivalry any of us care about when we're four. But by the last week of December, I was starting to panic. The NFL owners were threatening a lockout, the rich old man version of taking your ball and going home. If I didn't cover a game in the next two weeks, there might not be any games in 2011 to see[1], and with a quick glance at the NFL schedule I realized the Cowboys and Redskins had already played for the last time that season. As I began to wonder whether my readers would believe the Texans and Jaguars were the most heated rivalry in the NFL, I noticed the Green Bay Pack-

---

1. In case some of you get your news only from my books, the 2011 season did take place. Also, Osama bin Laden was killed, Prince William got married, and Charlie Sheen had a crazy spell.

ers and Chicago Bears had yet to play each other for the second time. An online search confirmed the Bears and Packers did, in fact, hate each other's guts. They've hated each other longer than any other two teams in the NFL. Only problem was I had to go to Green Bay in January.

~~~

The NFL looked a lot different when it began as the American Professional Football Association on September 17, 1920. You probably wouldn't recognize any of the ten teams that two years later would be called the National Football League. The Akron Professionals sound more like a temp agency than a football team. The Professionals folded in 1927, so in a way I guess they were a temp agency. Who can forget the Columbus Panhandles? The team you'd try not to make eye contact with when they asked you for spare change. Only two of the original teams are still around today. The Chicago Cardinals, who moved to St. Louis, then moved again to Arizona, and the Decatur Staleys, who moved to Chicago and changed their name to the slightly more intimidating Bears. The Green Bay Packers joined the league one year later, and on November 27, 1921, the Bears and Packers played for the first time. The Bears won, 20–0.

Since that first game, the teams have played 184 times, by far the longest running NFL rivalry. Because the teams are in the same division, they always play twice each season, plus possible playoff match-ups. Despite each team's success though, the Bears and Packers met only once in the playoffs before 2010, a 33–14 game won by the Bears in 1941, but more on that in a bit.

~~~

My journey to Green Bay began early on New Year's Day from Hammond, Indiana. After a quick breakfast, I was in the car, headed north toward the frozen tundra. It's about a five-hour drive, and I figured I would spend the rest of the day exploring the Packers' home. My route took me through Chicago for the first time. I struggled to stay in my lane while I craned my neck for a better look at the incredible skyline. I am not a well-traveled person. Starting this project, I had spent only thirty-one days outside the southeastern United States, and I'm thirty-three years old. When I see a big city like Chicago or Milwaukee, which I drove through next, I'm struck with childlike wonder. Okay, maybe not Milwaukee.

Closer to Green Bay, I saw more and more snow. It occurred to me that this wasn't recent snow, but snow from days and weeks ago that hadn't melted. Mind-boggling for a boy from Alabama. Growing up we got snow once a year, twice if we were lucky. With one exception,[2] the snow always melted into a cold, muddy soup by lunchtime.

About twenty miles south of Green Bay, I pulled off the interstate to fill up. I assumed it was cold outside but figured I could handle it in my jeans and sweatshirt for the three minutes it would take to fill a Honda Accord. Stepping out of the car, I was struck by the most unholy wind that has ever blown across the face of the earth. I fumbled with the gas cap, struggled to insert my credit card into the pump, set the lock on the nozzle, and leapt back into my car and screamed.

The temperature was in the teens, but a twenty-mile-per-hour wind made it feel like ten below death. I'd spent maybe fifty seconds outside, and now back in the car my face exploded into a thousand tiny pinpricks as it thawed. Somehow my hair hurt. It was the first of many times I questioned the sanity of people who willingly live in Wisconsin.

I explored Green Bay from the driver's seat, the heat on full blast. I saw a frozen river. Not a pond, but a river, frozen solid. The only time I ventured outside was to run into the Packers team store connected to Lambeau Field. I had to buy one of those cheese heads you see on television. At that point, I debated whether I was going to attend the next day's game. I figured I could sell the ticket, watch the game from the comfort of my

---

2. I survived the Blizzard of '93.

hotel, make up a bunch of stuff, and none of you would be the wiser.

After a delicious steak dinner from the Titletown Brewing Co., I searched for a Walmart. I needed to buy some boots because my New Balances would not cut it at tomorrow's game. Walking in, I passed a woman leaving with a handful of poster board paper. As soon as she cleared the doors, the wind ripped the poster boards from her hand and threw them thousands of feet into the air, never to be seen again. She turned and walked back inside, almost like she'd expected it to happen. When I walked outside ten minutes later, I was hit by the same wind and said things better left unprinted. In my defense, it is nearly impossible to walk into a negative ten–degree wind chill and not curse.

~~~

The night before the game, I read about the Bears–Packers rivalry in Gary D'Amato and Cliff Christl's book *Mudbaths and Bloodbaths*, which I'd mistakenly bought thinking the title was *Mudbloods and Bloodbaths* and it had something to do with Harry Potter.

Starting out, my contention was that rivalries are fan driven. In the rivalry I know best, Alabama–Auburn, the players seem to have a grip on things following the game. The weeping and gnashing of teeth happen in the stands. I figured the NFL would be the same, maybe worse. The players are professionals, so they play for the money, not the logo on their helmet. How could rivalries mean anything when free agency could have them playing on that rival team at some point? I could not have been more wrong.

I learned that with the Bears and the Packers, the hate was there from the beginning. It started with the Bears' first coach, George "Papa Bear" Halas, and the Packers' first coach, Earl "Curly" Lambeau. The two wouldn't even shake hands after a game. "Shake hands! That would have been a lie," Lambeau once said. "If I lost, I wanted to punch Halas in the nose. If he lost, Halas wanted to punch me."

For the patriarchal coaches, nothing mattered more than beating the other. Part of it was utter contempt, but it also had to do with championships. Either the Bears or the Packers won nearly half of the pre–Super Bowl NFL championships. If Lambeau or Halas wanted a ring, it usually meant going through the other to get it.

Between Halas and Lambeau were allegations of cheating, spying, and sabotage. Lambeau resigned as Packers coach in 1949, but Halas' distrust of all things Green Bay extended all the way to Curly's most famous successor, the great Vince Lombardi. Halas believed Lombardi had bugged the visitor's locker room in Green Bay, so he gave fake pregame speeches to his team, only giving his real instructions on the ramp down to the field.

As much as these teams hated and distrusted each other, they realized early that their survival might depend on each other. Seven days after the attack on Pearl Harbor, the Packers and Bears met for the NFL's Western Division championship. There were 43,425 fans in attendance. The next week, when the victorious Bears hosted the NFL championship, the game drew only 13,341. This probably explains why, fifteen years later, George Halas spoke at a rally to urge the citizens of Green Bay to build a new stadium for the Packers. Without the new stadium, which would later be named Lambeau Field, the Packers would have probably gone the way of the Professionals and Panhandles. Instead, Green Bay is still the smallest American city with a major professional sports franchise.

As I read late into the evening, I had to laugh at a chapter titled "Violence, Venom, and Villains." It sounded like poisonous mobsters, not football players. Another chapter covered seven men who "wielded vicious forearms and nasty attitudes." Guys with names like Butkus, Nagurski, Nitschke, and Ditka. It's a different kind of rivalry when the guys who break bones are more celebrated than the guys who score touchdowns. Now I wondered if the intensity in the stands could ever match the intensity on the field.

~~~

The next morning I put on the following articles of clothing: A pair of dress socks, a pair of athletic socks, a pair of super-thermal Under Armour snow ski socks. Boxers, a pair of long thermal underwear, pajama pants, and blue jeans. An I-can't-breathe-this-is-so-tight long-sleeved thermal shirt designed for arctic exploration, a long-sleeved T-shirt, a fleece pullover, and the thickest coat I own. Topped off with construction boots, ski gloves, a scarf, and a toboggan[3], I was ready to face the day. Of course it was about this time I realized I had to pee.

I arrived at Lambeau Field around 10:00 a.m., which would have been great if the game started at noon like I thought, but NFL flex scheduling pushed kickoff to 3:30 p.m. without consulting me. I had a lot of time to kill, and a lot of clothes on. But even the layers didn't keep me warm, particularly not the twenty-dollar boots covering my nearly frost-bitten feet. However I was way overdressed to spend the day inside, which is where I wound up, sitting in a deserted corner of the Lambeau Field Atrium atop a pile of my clothing.

A couple of Bears fans ate lunch next to me, and we talked about the rivalry. "We've been coming up here for years," one of them said. "It's a nice place to watch football, and the people are friendly." This wasn't the material I wanted, so I asked, "Do you guys root for the Packers when they aren't playing the Bears?"

"Of course not," said the other man. "He said they were friendly, he didn't say we like them. That being said, hating them isn't nearly as fun right now because they're too busy hating Brett Favre to return our affections."

Truer words may have never been spoken. Favre left the

---

3. My editor believes some clarification is needed here. In the south, a lot of people call winter caps 'toboggans'. Everywhere else, a toboggan is a sled. I did not have a sled on my head.

Packers three seasons prior, and still Green Bay fans talked about him with a disdain generally reserved for war criminals. Professional sports fans hate their rivals, but not nearly as much as they hate players who have spurned them.

After lunch, I bundled back up and ventured out for a walk around Lambeau Field. If you were to drop from the sky two blocks from the stadium, assuming you survived the fall, you wouldn't believe an NFL team plays games in this neighborhood. It feels like you are on the set of *The Wonder Years*. Tidy little houses with neat little yards, each porch home to a Packers flag. The homes just across Lombardi Avenue even have yellow and green fences, one delivering the message "In McCarthy We Trust."[4]

Sports fans commonly exhibit a sense of ownership when talking about their favorite team. This may be more prevalent in the college game, particularly with graduates of a school, but it pervades all sports. I refer to Auburn's football team as "we," although first-person plural is probably not the best way to describe a team I do not play for. Green Bay fans display this sense of ownership too, but they actually own the team.

The Green Bay Packers are the only community-owned, non-profit franchise in American professional sports: 112,015 people, owning 4,750,934 shares, lay claim to the team's ownership. The shareholders elect a board of directors, who in turn elect a seven-member executive committee, who in turn join forces to fight super villains[5]. So when Packers fans say "we," they've got the stock certificate on their wall to prove it.

It seemed most of the Packers' owners were out in the Lambeau parking lot. I didn't expect a big tailgating scene with temperatures in the teens, but the parking lot was full of men, women, and children huddled around grills, apparently having a dandy time. I saw a sign informing tailgaters that garbage can fires were restricted, to distinguish the parking lot from a home-

---

4. I assume Mike, not Joseph, although this state did elect the latter twice.
5. I may be thinking about *The Avengers*.

less camp, I suppose. I continued to question the sanity of the people who willingly live here.

~~~

The game could not have been bigger, at least not for Green Bay. The Packers' only chance to make the NFL playoffs was to beat their rival in this, the last game of the regular season. The Bears had already clinched the second seed in the NFC, and except for their hatred of all things green and yellow, they had little to play for. There were even discussions of whether Chicago coach Lovie Smith would sit his starters to guard against injuries.

I took my seat near the north end zone during warm-ups and was confused to see the pregame music being mixed on turntables by an on-field DJ. Not quite a marching band, but to each his own. As entertaining as it is to watch men stretch to rap music, I was freezing and went back inside for a few more minutes of warmth. When I returned, shortly before kickoff, my seat had disappeared. Seems everyone in the stadium was dressed as warmly as I was, making us all twice normal size. I found a small crevice between the two people I assumed were supposed to be on either side of me and wedged myself in.

Behind me I could hear a guy arguing with his girlfriend that she should go pee now, before the game. She insisted she didn't have to go, and she did hold it until the third play of the game. About this time the PA announcer gave the game-time temperature of nineteen degrees. People cheered and laughed, and one man yelled, "Heat wave!"

No one scored in the first quarter. I know it's not the case, but my memory consists only of one-yard runs up the middle. I don't know how anyone could throw or catch a football in that cold; it seems like they would want to run up the middle to find warmth in the scrums. Between quarters, two very late arriving Bears fans joined the row below me. One, a monster of a man in a Bronko Nagurski jersey, kept yelling, "Please pardon my Bears jersey," to a chorus of boos from the Packers faithful in our section.

I turned to the Packers fan to my right and said, "I wish I was as big as that guy, those extra pounds probably keep him pretty warm."

"No, you're better off being skinny, less of you to be cold."

This must be the famous midwestern sensibility you always hear about.

The Bears' Robbie Gould kicked a field goal in the second quarter. I assume his foot was solid blue the next morning. Doctors may have amputated it. Halftime came, and a drum line took the field, beating out a rhythm that matched my chattering teeth. A man was pulled from the crowd and given a chance to catch footballs shot miles into the air by some sort of football launching machine. He caught the first one, and I kid you not, won a snow blower.

Late in the third quarter, the Packers' Mason Crosby kicked a field goal of his own, and we were tied at three. Every part of me began to fear overtime. I knew an extra fifteen minutes in that weather would probably cost me my fingers. I turned again to the man next to me and kindly asked if he would set my hair on fire. "You'll just end up bald, and then your head will be colder."

Throughout the game I occasionally scanned the crowd in hopes of catching a verbal or, better yet, physical altercation I could write about. I never saw the latter, but at almost any point in the game, I could spot a Bears and Packers fan screaming at each other. These fights almost always resolved by one of the two saying something that made the other laugh, and they would both sit down.

When I asked Rick Eby, a Bears fan living in Wisconsin (which makes me double question his sanity), about altercations with opposing fans, he told me, "I've been involved in some friendly banter at Lambeau Field, but there is a love/hate relationship with the fans that generates a level of respect."

A few weeks later, I talked to Gary D'Amato, co-author

of *Mudbaths and Bloodbaths* and sports writer for the *Milwaukee Journal Sentinel*. When I told him about this, he wasn't surprised. "It's probably good natured for the most part," he told me. "But when you mix booze with a rivalry, two guys can say the wrong thing. I'd guess there are more instances of fighting at the Packers–Bears games than any other." It wasn't hard to find articles detailing numerous arrests at the Packers–Bears games, including twelve from this game. I was just sitting in the wrong section.

Gary was the second person to mention the effect alcohol has on fans. We've all seen alcohol magnify emotions, from the angry drunk who picks fights with everyone to the "I love you" guy who hugs everyone in sight. Rivalry games provide the most emotionally charged atmosphere in sports. When you combine that with alcohol, you see guys leaving the game in handcuffs. Of course alcohol also helps create these emotionally charged atmospheres we love so much, so what can you do? As Homer Simpson once said, "Here's to alcohol: the cause of, and solution to, all of life's problems."

At this point, it seemed neither team wanted to make the mistake that would give the other the win. Early in the fourth quarter, the Packers had the ball, third and three at their own thirty-three-yard line. Folks around me resigned themselves to another three and out with a punt, but Aaron Rogers hit Donald Driver for twenty-one yards. The next play, Rogers hit Greg Jennings for forty-six yards, down to the Chicago one-yard line. Then Rogers dumped a pass over the top to Donald Lee for a Green Bay touchdown. Seventy thousand Packers fans released three hours of emotion, and Lambeau field began to shake. Lee spiked the ball, flexed, and leapt into the waiting arms of the Packers faithful. How could you not feel ownership of your team when they celebrate touchdowns with you in the stands?

The Bears squandered their next two possessions, then took the ball for the last time with 4:49 left to play on their own two-yard line. Quarterback Jay Cutler, who had looked pretty blah all day, was now finding his receivers, and before we knew it the Bears were down to the Green Bay thirty-two. But Cutler's final pass was intercepted by Nick Collins, and it was all over. The Packers were going to the playoffs. Many of the Green Bay players circled the field, thanking their shareholders, while I hobbled on numb feet to my car.

~~~

After the game, I drove south toward Chicago, and somewhere near Sheboygan I began to feel my toes again. I had sports talk on the radio, and most were praising Lovie Smith for playing his starters, although many of the Bears players admitted the game didn't mean that much to them. Brian Urlacher, the heart and soul of the Bears' defense, said, "We weren't playing for anything," then went on to say the contest didn't feel like a playoff game.

Does this mean Urlacher and the other Bears didn't play as hard as they could have? I suspect it might, which is understandable, since their playoff fate was already decided. But I can't picture Dick Butkus not giving his all against the Packers just because the second seed in the NFC was already clinched.

Mark Twain once said, "I was seldom able to see an opportunity until it had ceased to be one." The Bears know now the opportunity they had that frigid afternoon in Green Bay, because three weeks later a very confident Packers team strolled into Chicago to face the Bears in the NFC championship game. Once again, Green Bay defeated Chicago, 21–14, this time advancing to the Super Bowl, where they beat the Pittsburgh Steelers to claim the Lombardi Trophy.

~~~

I spoke to Ted Medinger, a Packers fan from Holmen, Wisconsin, sometime after the Super Bowl and asked him if he ever feels the need to reexamine his level of animosity toward the Bears. "Sure," he said. "Especially after a loss. I'll say something dumb and try to remember that life goes on. Just tip your hat, and congratulate them. That being said, without these emotions, sports wouldn't be nearly as fun."

Sports wouldn't be as fun without the emotions. I'm sure some Bears fans wish right now that the Packers had folded back in the 1940s. I know many college fans want their rival team to get the NCAA death penalty. The truth is, these rivalries are the reason many of us care so much. Believe it or not, losing your rival would be much worse than losing *to* your rival.

Ted agreed. "Losing the Bears would definitely take away from the game. Bears week is extra special, and for so many the anticipation of a rivalry game is the best part. I would never want to lose that, and I don't think the Bears would either."

All year I tried to get opposing fans to say something they like about their rival. The best that Jason Spitzer, a Packers fan from Milwaukee, could come up with is, "I like that the Bears are in Illinois, and not in Wisconsin." And I get it; I'm no better when it comes to the Crimson Tide. But maybe the next time we see a fan of our rival team, instead of wishing ill will, we can stop and remember that sports wouldn't be nearly as fun without them.

Celtics vs. Lakers

Staples Center – Los Angeles, California
January 30, 2011

Racism is man's gravest threat to man—the maximum of hatred for a minimum of reason.
—Abraham J. Heschel

I am not a seasoned air traveler. This became frighteningly clear on my drive to Atlanta's Hartsfield Airport the morning of January 29th, when I realized I'd never flown without Tricia sitting next to me, squeezing my hand, and explaining that every noise I heard was not one of the plane's wings falling off. Hyperventilating, I pulled over and pondered turning around and driving the thirty-four hours from Auburn to Los Angeles, but I decided if I'm going to write this book, I'm going to have to get used to flying. Besides, I was leaving for Scotland in three weeks, and driving there would prove difficult.

I think I would have been okay had Tricia and I not just begun re-watching the first season of *Lost*. Episodes one and two are pretty heavy on graphic plane crash sequences, and knowing my seat location for the flight to LAX,[1] I was either going to be a "tailie" or be sucked out of the plane into oblivion. Once on board, I scanned the plane for a great ensemble cast. If there had been an Iraqi, a couple of Koreans, a 400-pound lottery winner, and a spinal surgeon on board, I'd have popped the emergency

---

1. You know where Oceanic Flight 815 was heading? That's right, LAX.

hatch and run for my life. Thankfully it was just me and a boring bunch of white people flying across the country. I wondered if I was the only one going to see the Lakers and Celtics play.

~~~

When I think of the 1980s, I think of *Thriller*, Rubik's Cubes, New Coke, Bill Cosby sweaters, and the Lakers–Celtics rivalry. In my mind, those teams played in the NBA finals every year from 1980 to 1989, each series going seven games, and each game coming down to a last second shot. In reality the squads met in the finals only three times, with the Celtics winning in 1984 and the Lakers winning in '85 and '87. But either the Lakers or Celtics did play in every NBA final from 1980 to 1989, and these teams did win eight of the ten championships from that fashion nightmare of a decade. When EA Sports released the first NBA-endorsed video basketball game in 1989, it wasn't called NBA 1989, it was called Lakers vs. Celtics—and I would crush you if we ever played.

The Lakers and Celtics were led throughout the eighties by their respective superstars, Magic Johnson and Larry Bird, the men credited with saving basketball.[2] Their personal rivalry began a year earlier, in 1979, when they met in the NCAA championship game, with Magic's Michigan State Spartans beating Bird's Indiana State Sycamores, 75–64. With the Celtics, Bird won three consecutive NBA MVP awards from 1984–1986. Magic won the MVP three times as well, in 1987, 1989, and 1990. The two combined for twenty-four NBA all-star appearances (twelve each), five NBA finals MVPs, and one very cheesy Converse commercial. Oh, and by the way, Bird is white and Magic is black.

In the 1980s, Lakers vs. Celtics became more than a basketball game; it grew to symbolize America's racial identity. The Lakers were black, apart from Kurt Rambis, who was so stereotypically white he made the other Lakers somehow blacker. In

---

2. From what, I do not know. Maybe an asteroid?

contrast, the Celtics could not have been whiter. Find any team photo from the eighties and 75 percent of the players will be white, this in a league that was 80 percent black.

I suppose it was more than that. LA was flashy, and in the eighties black people apparently loved flashy things, like behind-the-back passes and parachute pants. Boston was the dorky team, and white people in the eighties loved dorky things, like bounce passes and *Star Wars*. The reality was, if you were white in the 1980s, you loved the Celtics, because they looked like you, and they appreciated science fiction. And if you were black, well, you didn't necessarily have to love the Lakers, but you had to hate the Celtics, even if you lived in Boston.

ESPN's Howard Bryant said, "Black kids in Boston were taken by Julius Erving and the Philadelphia 76ers. It was no different in Plymouth, where the handful of African Americans and Cape Verdeans rooted for the Sixers and the Lakers (and later the Detroit Pistons, but never the Celtics). The Celtics were the white fan's team."

When we create idols, we tend to create them in our image. Maybe there is nothing wrong with white suburban kids hanging Larry Bird posters on their walls because Larry Bird looked like them,[3] and maybe there is nothing wrong with black kids in Boston spurning the hometown Celtics for Dr. J, but are there dangers to this way of thinking? It would generally be frowned upon for me to root against a player because he is black. Is it any different rooting for a player because he is white?

~~~

If you read *God and Football*, you probably (a) are related to me and (b) remember Alicia and Russell Clayton, my Chick-fil-A loving friends from Oxford, Mississippi. They wanted to be reoccurring characters in my work and met me in LA the day before the game. When I called Russell from the airport, he said they were headed to Santa Monica Pier, so I whistled for a cab, and when

---

3. Assuming they had a big nose and a blonde afro-mullet.

it came near, the license plate said "Fresh" and it had dice in the mirror.

It's funny how nervous I was about flying, which statistically is a pretty safe way to travel, compared with how calm I was on that cab ride, which involved a lot of swerving and screeching, all at speeds reserved for cars with sponsors on their hoods. There is a certain detachment when riding in cabs; it almost feels like you are watching someone else play a video game, and sure enough, it got me to Santa Monica safe, sound, and significantly lighter in wallet. It was time to see LA.

I met Russell and Alicia near the end of the pier but refused to hug them or even shake hands. The night before they'd scored tickets to the *Tonight Show with Jay Leno*, where they came in contact with none other than Justin Bieber, undoubtedly contracting the fever that shares his name. So I said hello from a safe distance, and we were off to explore.

I'm a Gulf Coast guy, so seeing the ocean and mountains at the same time is visually confusing for me, as is an amusement park on a pier, but this little part of the world is truly gorgeous and certainly worthy of all the postcards it produces. We stayed in Santa Monica until we saw the tenth muscle-bound guy in a bikini bottom, which exceeded my daily limit, then we drove to Rodeo Drive for lunch.

~~~

Russell and I didn't see any Lakers fans in Santa Monica, and as we fought through Saturday afternoon traffic, we talked about the Los Angeles sports scene. There is so much going on in a city this big. Sports fans have an overwhelming number of choices. LA is home to the Dodgers, Angels, Kings, Galaxy, Lakers, Clippers, USC, UCLA, among others. It would take something incredibly big to grab this city's attention, and I began to doubt a regular season game between the Lakers and Celtics was enough.

I spoke to Cheryl Fletcher, a community life pastor at Christian Assembly in Eagle Rock, just north of LA. A Lakers fan who admits the team's colors are a little hard for a girl to get behind, Cheryl grew up in Redlands, California, but went to Texas for college and lived there for sixteen years. We talked about living in a college town, as opposed to one of the largest cities in the world. "In Austin, when there was a home football game, you experienced it whether you wanted to or not. Here, if you are not into sports, you only experience it as traffic. You'll be driving along on a Saturday, when all of a sudden you're like, 'What the?!' And then a car with a Dodgers flag will drive by and you realize what's going on."

Cheryl said it's hard for any one thing to captivate the entire city, but when the Lakers reach the NBA finals, they do just that. "When they are in the finals, everyone is watching. Everyone is into it."

The Lakers are a big fish in a big pond, but what about a rivalry where the two teams are separated by three thousand miles? The best rivalries in sports are almost all regional, if not local. Duke and UNC are eight miles apart. Ohio State and University of Michigan share a border. USC and UCLA share a city. This proximity brings fans from each team into contact on a daily basis, at work, or church, or sometimes around the family dinner table. Constant fan interaction truly makes a rivalry intense. It's hard to imagine Lakers and Celtics fans arguing over the Thanksgiving turkey, because for the most part they don't know each other.

I asked Lakers fan Javier Entrekin about this, and the only Celtics fan he knew was his FedEx guy, a Celtics fan born and raised in LA. When I asked Dan White, a Celtics fan, if he'd had any altercations with Lakers fans in the past, he told me, "I'm not sure if I've ever even met a true Lakers fan in person."

DJ Sims, another Boston fan, doesn't come across many Lakers fans either, but that doesn't mean he likes them. "I hate them. Hate their guts. Not just the fans, not just the players, but the organization as a whole, all the way from Magic down to the kids that dry sweat off the floor. In no way is it a joke." I asked DJ if he ever feels the need to reexamine this hate, perhaps in light of his religious beliefs, and he said, "I'm sure if Jesus were around today he'd hate LA as well."

I asked DJ if distance hurt the rivalry, and he said, "In some ways it does; however, it does add a little something extra because when you finally do see them, you want to make sure they know you hate them, their team, their city, their momma, their brothers, their sisters, dogs, cats, their everything."

Perhaps I was wrong. Distance didn't lessen the hate during the Cold War either. Maybe not knowing your rival makes it easier to demonize them and, according to DJ, their mommas.

~~~

Living in Auburn, I don't see many Lamborghinis. On Rodeo Drive, we saw five in ten minutes, not to mention Ferraris, Bentleys, Maseratis, and Alfa Romeos. In Los Angeles it's possible to rent them for around $200 an hour. Want to impress your lunch date? Show up in a Ferrari. Tell her you wrecked it when you pick her up in your Camry the next time.

We lunched at the Urth Café, an organic coffee company in Beverly Hills, then walked up and down Rodeo Drive, peeking inside Gucci, Prada, and Dior, making sure to turn away before a sales associate caught our eye, just in case it cost money to look. For someone who primarily shops at Old Navy, the experience was intimidating.

From there we loaded up on Sprinkles Cupcakes, then decided it was time to see the famed Hollywood sign. We drove down Sunset Boulevard, resisting the urge to sing Sheryl Crow songs, and weaved our way up the Hollywood Hills.

At this point, I wasn't entirely sold on Los Angeles. Air I can see and shops I can't afford are not high on the list of things I look for in a city. But once I got out of the car, high up in those green hills, with the sun setting over the Pacific, and the cool breeze blowing across my face, it became one of my new favorite places on earth. If Tricia and I had $3.9 million, we'd buy a house there tomorrow.

For dinner we ate at In-N-Out Burger. Russell and Alicia had already eaten there three times before I arrived, continuing their slight obsession with Christian-owned fast-food joints.[4] Before driving back to our hotel, we stopped by High Voltage Tattoo, the parlor featured on the show *LA Ink*. I've never seen the show, but Russell and Alicia are fans. We stepped inside for a moment, and I resisted the urge to have "Gibbs" written across my upper back in Olde English.

Sunday morning dawned cold and rainy, which was completely unacceptable for southern California, even in January. I called home, and Tricia informed me that it was seventy and sunny. I was in a bad mood as we fought bumper-to-bumper Sunday midmorning traffic on our way to the Staples Center.

~~~

Twenty years from now no one will write about how the 2010–11 Lakers–Celtics rivalry was a mirror of race relations in the United States. Going into this particular game it was the Lakers who actually had two white Americans (Steve Blake and Luke Walton) compared to the Celtics' one (Troy Murphy). These days, if a white supremacist cheers for the Celtics, he or she is one tolerant white supremacist.[5] But in the eighties it was said that Boston was the white fan's team. Bob Ryan of the *Boston Globe* told Chuck Klosterman for his essay on the rivalry that "the Celtics were clearly the team of blatant racists. And that's no fault of the Celtics. But the fact that they had so many great white players made them heroes to racists and people in the Deep South. Even in Boston, there was an element of their fandom that was very

---

4. In-N-Out Burger discretely prints Bible verses on the bottom of their soda cups, reflecting the Christian beliefs of its founders, Harry and Esther Snyder.

5. White supremacists would probably prefer the All-American Basketball Alliance, a planned all-white league created by Atlanta businessman Don "Moose" Lewis. Lewis wanted to create the AABA because he felt white people should be given their own league to play "fundamental basketball, which they like" instead of the "street ball" he said is played by nonwhites. Black and white peopled agreed this was about the stupidest idea they'd ever heard.

happy they had white superstars. Anybody who would deny that is naive."

Ryan makes it sound like white fans rooting for white NBA players are racists, but I don't think every white kid who wore a Bird jersey also had a Klan robe in their closet. I asked my Twitter followers what they thought, and some agreed with Ryan. Others saw nothing wrong with wanting your heroes to look like you, citing the great number of African Americans turned on to golf by Tigers Woods. One follower pointed out that if whites are the minority in a sport, then you are actually rooting for diversity. Everyone agreed you couldn't cheer for Jeff Gordon because he is white.

I talked to Marcus "Goodie" Goodloe, a pastor on staff at Mosaic, a multi-site church based in LA, and former QB for the New Mexico Lobos. Goodie described himself as a bit of a radical Lakers fan, admitting he will not watch SportsCenter or listen to talk radio for weeks after the Lakers exit the playoffs.

Goodie said he didn't think it was wrong for kids, inner city or otherwise, to look for a sports hero or icon they can identify with. He went on to say, "I think when it becomes inappropriate or wrong is when there is some idea of supremacy based on the color of a person's skin."

Perhaps age has something to do with it. A ten-year-old white kid could look to Larry Bird as a role model and think, "This guy looks like me, and if he made it to the NBA, so can I." Black kids could do the same with Tiger. But when you hear a fifty-year-old man say, "I cheer for Larry Bird because he is white," it sounds a little more sinister.

~~~

Even if the Lakers and Celtics don't symbolize all they once did, the rivalry is once again white hot, after a nearly two-decade hiatus. In 2008, the teams met in the NBA finals for the first time since 1987, with the Celtics winning the title in six games. Two years later, the old foes met again, this time with the Lakers winning in seven. Today's game would be their first matchup of the season and the first since that epic game seven.

We arrived early and huddled under an awning near a giant statue of Magic Johnson to stay dry. Once the gates opened, we rushed inside and were handed towels that read, "Beat Boston." I used mine to dry my hair. We saw a handful of Boston fans milling around before the game and even saw one man in a Kobe Bryant jersey holding hands with a woman in a Kevin Garnett jersey. This nauseated everyone a bit.

Seeing a Lakers game in the Staples Center is a little like going to a movie. "Showtime" may have died with the eighties, but the team still clings to that persona. The tunnels from the concourse to the arena are lined with dark curtains, giving the place a movie theatre feel. Inside, the court is brightly lit, while the seating area is dark. It's obvious you are in store for a show.

Just before tip-off the stars begin to appear. Two we could spot right away, even from our seats near the ceiling, were Jack Nicholson and Matt Damon. Nicholson is always there, courtside, next to the visitor's bench. I'm not sure how often Damon attends, but the Boston-born actor was definitely cheering for the visitors. Russell and I checked StubHub for prices on those courtside seats; four were available for just over $20,000 each, but we opted for the top row of the upper level instead.

The Celtics were introduced to loud boos, the loudest reserved for Shaquille O'Neal. A man on the end of our row screamed "traitor" as loud as he could. O'Neal has played for four teams since leaving LA in 2004, but seeing your former superstar suiting up for your rival is hard to swallow. This cemented my belief that professional fans don't hate their rivals nearly as much as they hate their former players.

Boston led 22–21 after one quarter, and midway through the second Pau Gasol accidentally elbowed KG in the head. You could see the blood from our seats, and I'd wager the massive Band-Aid they put on Garnett's head could be seen from space. At the half, the Lakers had regained the lead, 54–50.

NBA crowds are often maligned as dull, but the Staples Center atmosphere was pretty rowdy, especially considering the game didn't mean much, apart from pride. Chants of "Boston sucks" filled the arena from time to time, and one of the largest ovations came when the video screen showed a young fan wearing a shirt that read "I hate Boston." Sure, there are kiss cams and Lakers Girls and the crowd is about as far from an English soccer mob as you can get, but the Celtics were in town, and folks were fired up. My favorite touch, something I imagine is unique to the Lakers, was a pep band perched high above the court in Section 308. An offshoot of the USC Trojan marching band, the Lakers band creates an atmosphere that's half college basketball, half late night talk show, but all LA.

The second half was all Paul Pierce as the Celtics forward scored seventeen of his thirty-two points, and the Celtics pulled away to win 109–96, despite Kobe Bryant's game-high forty-one points. As the clock wound down, Jack Nicholson left his seat, shaking hands with Celtics coach Doc Rivers as he passed.

After the game we fought our way outside, eventually running into a mass of people screaming and jockeying for position. Matt Damon and pals were exiting the Staples Center right in front of us, while Lakers fans cheered and begged for autographs. Only in Los Angeles could a guy spend two hours cheering not only against the home team but for the team's bitter rival, and afterwards the home fans still try to get his autograph. I bet if Jack Nicholson went to Boston they'd throw him in the harbor.

After the game we went to Grauman's Chinese Theatre, a Hollywood shrine to cement vandalism. After buying a few over-priced souvenirs, we took a van tour of celebrity homes. Piled into a van with about ten other suckers customers, we were off. Our guide sounded like an extra from a Cheech and Chong film, and within minutes we knew we'd made a mistake.

"To your right," he said over the van's PA system, "is the

house where actress Nicole Richie used to live."

"Can we get our $43 back?"

"No. Now if you will look to your left you will see a large row of shrubbery, and behind that shrubbery is the home of Laurence Fishburne's agent."

"Please, just let us out of the van. You can keep our money."

"No. Now, up ahead you will see a gate. Behind that gate, and up a long driveway, lives an actress from a nineties sitcom, but her name escapes me at the moment."

After the tour, which included a home recently repossessed from Nicolas Cage, we drove out to Diddy Riese Cookies, a shop near UCLA that specializes in gobs of ice cream stuffed between two fresh-baked cookies for only $1.50. With stomachs full, we fought bumper-to-bumper Sunday night traffic back to our hotel. I love LA.

~~~

Buzz Bissinger, author of *Friday Night Lights*, says he makes a point these days to ask white sports fans if they watch the NBA, and almost all say they once watched but no longer do. Bissinger takes this to mean that they watched when Larry Bird and John Stockton were superstars, but now that Kevin Love is the best white American in the league, they're not interested. It almost feels racist to say you don't watch the NBA.

Bissinger points out that many white fans he encounters attribute the success of white athletes to work ethic and intelligence, while black athletes succeed purely on God-given skill. Spike Lee echoed those sentiments during an ESPN town hall meeting, saying, "The perception is we just roll out of the womb and dunk." This way of thinking is perpetuated by the media with code words. Black quarterbacks are "athletic," while white NBA players are "intelligent" and "hard working." It's not always racist, or hateful, but stereotypes based on race are not helpful. Besides, anyone who ever saw me play basketball knows that I was neither intelligent nor hard working.

Saying only whites cheered for the Celtics in the 1980s is really no different than saying white players in the NBA succeed on hard work. I grew up in the Deep South, where my good friend's very white father adored the Lakers. I know this because he nearly killed us when we recorded one of our mini-goal dunk contests over his copy of game four of the 1987 NBA finals. On the other hand, my grandpa James loved the Boston Celtics, but not because they were white. His favorite player on those eighties teams was Robert Parish.

To paint Boston as the white man's team does a disservice to the Celtics' history. It was Boston that first drafted a black player, Chuck Cooper. It was Boston that first fielded an all-black starting five. And it was Boston that hired Bill Russell to be the first black head coach in NBA history.

~~~

Webster's defines racism as "a belief that race is the primary determinant of human traits and capacities and that racial differences produce an inherent superiority of a particular race."

Using that definition, white fans cheering for white players because they are white isn't necessarily racist, unless they believe whiteness produces an inherent superiority in basketball, which I cannot imagine anyone believes.[6] It's more of an identity issue, which perhaps is creating an Us vs. Them dynamic.

In his book *Why We Hate*, Rush W. Dozier Jr. says, "The distinction between us and them, however, does not completely coincide with hate." But Dozier goes on to say, "Even when hate is not involved, the us-them binary division has a formidable ability to turn off our empathy."

America has come a long way on race, but it still has far to go. If we continue to think of another race as "them," even if we harbor no ill will, at best we are just spinning our wheels. The Jews and Samaritans weren't necessarily on great terms during

---

6. Although saying African Americans are better at basketball than whites is racist, even though it doesn't really feel racist when I say it.

Christ's day, but Jesus didn't see us and them; he saw only "we." We should all strive for that we.

Maybe we are getting closer. Let's assume all white people in the eighties cheered for the Celtics because of race. If nothing has changed, then white people today would all love Duke basketball. But from my experience, that isn't exactly the case.

.

North Carolina vs. Duke

Cameron Indoor Stadium – Durham, North Carolina
February 9, 2011

I hate them with perfect hatred.
—Psalm 139:22

With just over eight minutes to play in the first half of the 2003 Duke-North Carolina game, Tar Heels guard Jackie Manuel was fouled and stepped to the line to attempt two free throws. Just before the referee bounced Manuel the ball, the entire Duke student section, which usually does all they can to distract the shooter, quietly took their seats, and from their midst rose a single, gyrating guy wearing nothing but a blue speedo. Manuel, clearly (and understandably) shaken, missed both free throws. The crowd went wild, and the legend of Speedo Guy was born.

"Did I ever tell you I was in Divinity School with Speedo Guy?"

My friend Jason Cook and I were driving to Durham when he revealed this valuable piece of information.

"Wait, Speedo Guy was in Divinity School?"

"Yeah, he's now a pastor in Knoxville. You want his phone number?"

Of course I did, and soon I was talking to Rev. Patrick King, aka Speedo Guy.

Patrick told me the morning of that fateful day he and his fellow graduate students were lined up outside Cameron Indoor Stadium, in hopes of securing good seats for later that night. "I'd fallen asleep in my chair," Patrick said, "and my cousin came and woke me up, saying our buddy Dan Rhodes had a brilliant idea to distract Carolina players at the free throw line, and before I heard the idea, he needed me to agree to say yes. And I knew my cousin and Dan well enough that I was like, 'Alright, I'm up for whatever.'"

Patrick went on to say his friend Dan had been laying awake in bed the night before, just dreaming of ways to distract Carolina's free throw shooters, and the idea of a speedo-clad divinity student just came to him.

I began to wander what kind of rivalry keeps people up at night just dreaming of ways to distract free throw shooters, and more importantly, what kind of rivalry causes a man of the cloth to dance around in the least amount of cloth possible. If this isn't hate, it's got to be something close.

~~~

"Yes, it's real hate," said Tar Heels fan Brian McKeithan. "If I'm walking down the street and see someone in a Duke hat, I want to slap it off. I'd kick a puppy if it had a Duke shirt on." Brian doesn't go so far as to not associate with Duke fans, but admits, "I have a close friend who is a Duke fan, and we cannot talk about college basketball, because it always ends up with one of us red-faced, reaching for the other's neck, while our significant others look on in total annoyance."

I asked Matt Zechini, a Duke fan from Cary, North Carolina, if he would describe his feelings toward UNC as hate, or something less. "It's real hate," he said. I asked if he ever felt he should tone it down, and he replied, "I probably should, but I don't. Go to hell, Carolina!"

Conner, a Blue Devil from Texas, said he tosses the H-word around from time to time, "but to say I actually hate them would be an overstatement. I just like Carolina better when we are crushing them."

Many admitted they wouldn't marry a fan from the other school, although some calculating Tar Heels guys reasoned that marrying a Duke grad wouldn't be the end of the world, because she would probably come from money. One UNC fan told me he considered leaving his church the morning his priest declared their church a Duke church. Others were more reasonable, if not a little fatalistic. "I'm a Methodist," said one UNC fan. "And all Methodist ministers around here went to Duke. What can you do?"

I wondered if these fan bases might sometimes feel the need to scrutinize the level of dislike they feel toward one another.

"Why would I?" asked Angelo Sellers, a Tar Heel from Garner, North Carolina. "The fact that there are Duke fans makes me question God's wisdom in bestowing us with free will."

Dave Myers, a UNC fan in Tennessee, seemed equally sure he was on the right side of this rivalry, and his logic is hard to debate. "I find it hard to believe Jesus is up in Heaven screaming, 'Go Devils!'"

But Sabrina Sowders, a Carolina fan from Columbia, South Carolina, has tried to reexamine her feelings toward Duke, because, in her words, "I was so mad I was shaking after they beat us earlier this season." Sabrina blames her feelings on her competitive nature, and says, "I'm growing. I don't expect my competitiveness to just go away, but I'm growing in it." She even felt slightly remorseful for booing an eight-year-old girl in a Duke T-shirt earlier in the year.

Jason, a Tar Heels fan from Amarillo, echoed Sabrina's sentiments, saying, "Absolutely! I believe this is an ongoing process for me. I find myself yelling things at the TV during games that I would never yell in public or probably in any other situation in life. All this over a sport? Over a game? I find that pretty embarrassing."

Nothing new—rival fans hate each other, with a few of them stopping to consider the ramifications. I understand why Duke and Carolina might hate each other. They are rivals, and that's what rivals do. What I want to know is why the rest of the sports world hates Duke as well.

~~~

After basketball season, I asked my Twitter followers why they hate Duke. Keep in mind that my followers, for the most part, are SEC football fans, many of them Auburn and Alabama fans, and have almost no connection to Duke. Even so, the response was overwhelming.

They are nerds. They are pompous. They are too white. They are all from New Jersey[1]. They go to games only to earn extra credit. Their coach looks like a rat. They get all the calls. They flop. They are entitled. They are rich. They are spoiled. They are arrogant. They are pretentious. Their coach has a creepy little mouth.

A Duke fan replied that it would be hard for the Duke haters to explain their dislike, without admitting they were jealous.

Are all the Duke haters around the country really just jealous of Duke, or does the size of Mike Krzyzewski's mouth actually produce this much bile?

Jay Bilas, a former Duke player and current ESPN analyst, told Terrence Moore of the *Atlanta Journal Constitution* that, "For years, people hated Notre Dame football. For years, so this hatred is not unique to Duke. People don't hate [mediocre] teams."

Bilas explains Duke's side: people hate us because we win. But North Carolina has more national championships than Duke, more ACC championships than Duke, more Final Four appearances than Duke, more all-time wins than Duke, and the Tar Heels hold a thirty-game head-to-head advantage over the

---

1. This is an odd one, but I heard it a lot talking to Carolina fans. They seem convinced 90 percent of the Duke student body once lived next door to Snookie. Truth is, only 15 percent of the 6,504 Duke undergrads come from the seven Mid-Atlantic states. If those seven states break down evenly, we're talking about 139 students from New Jersey, all of them with six-pack abs.

Blue Devils. This begs the question, why doesn't everyone hate North Carolina?

Later, in his column titled "Why We Hate Duke," Terrence Moore pointed out the racial side of Duke hatred, citing Jalen Rose's now infamous ESPN *30 for 30* interview, in which the former Fab Five member said when it comes to black players, Duke recruits only "Uncle Toms."

Moore went on to say the Duke hatred has a racial element similar to Ali–Frazier, and that, "Nowadays, if you're black, and you play or cheer for Duke—let's just say you aren't exactly hugged by a segment of your peers. I've seen as much from my friends and relatives forever."

Maybe race plays a part, but what about the legions of white fans that hate Duke just as much? Just last chapter I wrote about how in the 1980's it was said that white fans cheered for the Boston Celtics because they had white superstars. I don't have statistics, but Duke certainly appears to be one of the whitest top-tier college basketball programs in the country, yet white fans despise them just as much as black fans do.

Moore says it's all about perception, and Duke bashers, himself included, perceive Duke players to be arrogant, while admitting that in the case of current Duke star Nolan Smith, that perception couldn't be further from the truth. The other perception is that Duke gets all the calls.

I don't know if they get *all* the calls, but Duke does take an awful lot of charges. I remember in 2001 a group of friends were watching the Duke–Arizona championship game in my apartment. Shane Battier took a charge early in the first half, and my friend Kyle, who has zero ties to Duke or Carolina or Arizona, became so enraged that he stormed out of my apartment, slamming the door so hard pictures fell from the walls.

Will Blythe, a former literary editor at *Esquire* and dyed-in-the-wool Tar Heels fan, wrote an entire book about his hatred of all things Duke. The book's title says it all: *To Hate Like This Is to*

Love Thy Rival

Be Happy Forever. Blythe's reasons for hating the Blue Devils all make sense to a fan with intimate knowledge of a great rivalry, but halfway through he hits on something that may explain why not just Tar Heels, but everyone else, hates Duke. That something: Dick Vitale.

Blythe says, "In the Cold War bilateralism of the Duke-Carolina rivalry, in which the friend of my enemy was my enemy, ESPN announcer Dick Vitale had earned my enmity and that of Carolina fans for his hyperventilating, on-air slobberfests on behalf of all things Duke."

Dick Vitale and ESPN may not be the only reason America hates Duke, but they certainly aren't helping. Everyone knows Duke is a remarkable program and that their student section is loud and clever, so Vitale doesn't need to remind us of this on an hourly basis, especially not in an excited tone usually reserved for alerting others the building is on fire. Blythe goes on to tell the story of some UNC students who invented a Dick Vitale drinking game. Every time Vitale mentions Duke, the students drink a beer. The catch: they play this game during contests not involving Duke. The students said they're usually drunk by halftime.

Why do people hate Duke? I don't know. Maybe arrogance, or too many white players, or not enough black players, or too many students from New Jersey, or the size of their coach's mouth. In the end, Duke is a perfect storm of loathing. That being said, I've always kind of liked them.

~~~

Jason and I drove most of the day from Birmingham to Chapel Hill, arriving at the home of Mitch Simpson after dinner. Mitch is the pastor of University Baptist Church in Chapel Hill, and he looks like the Baptist version of Dos Equis' Most Interesting Man in the World[2].

Mitch has been at University Baptist for twenty-one years, and in seven of those years either Duke or North Carolina won

---

2. I don't always drink beer, but when I do, I'd rather people not know.

the national championship. A lifelong Tar Heels fan, Mitch received his undergraduate degree from UNC but attended seminary at Duke. When I asked him about this, he smiled and said, "I went there as a missionary."

The next morning, Jason drove me to University Baptist Church, which is at the corner of Franklin and Columbia Street, Chapel Hill's version of Times Square. From there we walked around the UNC campus. Parts of campus are nearly as old as the United States, and as we strolled through tree-lined quads, I began to fall in love, which was odd considering the Duke T-shirt under my jacket.

I was born in Fayetteville, North Carolina. My dad joined the army out of high school, and my folks were stationed there for a few years. A year after I was born, Dad was out of the army and we moved back to Alabama, where I've lived ever since. And despite the fact that I've lived 98 percent of my life in Alabama, I've always been proud to hail from the Tar Heel State. I even used the seemingly arbitrary nature of military base assignments as an excuse to cheer for Duke. Though had dad been stationed at Fort William Henry Harrison, I doubt I would have cheered for the Montana Grizzlies.

However, with each step on the Carolina campus, my affection grew. Chapel Hill is your quintessential college town. Something about gnarly old trees hanging over stately old buildings leaves me smitten. Plus the students mostly wore Carolina Blue T-shirts and sweaters, and no one looks bad in that shade.

The bookstore had so much Carolina Blue that Jason started to feel sick, so he walked outside while I bought a mug with the UNC alma mater on it. Walking back to town, we passed the Old Well, perhaps Carolina's most famous campus landmark. Tradition holds that if you drink from the well on the first day of class, you will make straight As. I'm not sure what happens when someone who graduated eight years ago with a 2.7 GPA drinks from it, but I don't feel smarter.

Jason took me to lunch at a place called Mama Dips. To this day, if I think hard enough about their chicken and dumplings, I begin to drool. Then it was time to see Duke, so we got in the car, drove to Route 15-501, and before we could listen to "Stairway to Heaven" in its entirety, we pulled on to Duke's campus.

Jason took Chapel Drive, and as we rounded the corner, he cranked up the classical music on his stereo. The effect was surreal. Tricia and I had visited France that summer, and I felt transported back. The first thing I saw was the chapel, its bell tower stark against the Carolina sky. The surrounding buildings give no indication that you are still in the American South. The UNC campus reminded me a little of Auburn; Duke reminded me of an art history class.

We parked, and Jason started the tour. First the chapel, which is even more impressive inside. From there we walked through a maze of seemingly identical dormitories, occasionally passing students, prompting Jason to mumble, in his best Ogre impersonation, "Nerds!"

"Wait, you went to school here. Can you call them nerds?"

"I went to graduate school here," Jason said. "I can still make fun of undergrads."

Fair enough.

Finally it was time to see Cameron Indoor Stadium. If the buildings were not labeled, you'd only discover it by trial and error. On other campuses, you can spot the historic buildings, the new buildings, and the buildings that had the misfortune of being designed in the 1970s. At Duke, the campus is so uniform you cannot tell the basketball arena from a chemistry lab. Who knows, maybe it doubles as a chemistry lab during away games. But the thousands of students camping outside Cameron Indoor might be a tip.

Krzyzewskiville, as it is known, is in essence a tent city, not for refugees but for undergrads desperate to see Duke basketball. Like any city, K-ville has its laws—one person must always be with the tent, even during 2:00 a.m. rain storms when it's forty degrees out—but no one I saw looked upset they'd spent the last forty days living like a homeless person. This is one of the most over-exposed traditions in college sports, and UNC fans are sick of hearing about it, but it is pretty cool.

~~~

That evening Jason dropped me off back at Cameron, where the crowd swelled, waiting for the gates to open. I stood out of the way, but as the collective anxiety grew, I started to feel nervous for no reason. The Cameron Crazies were lined up just waiting to be unleashed, and once inside they would let loose a three-hour barrage of taunts. Occasionally a Carolina fan walked by and students chanted and extended one arm, hexing them as they passed.

Only a few Carolina fans were in Cameron Indoor that night, but college basketball doesn't exactly lend itself to away game travel. Compared with football, the seating capacity is small (9,200 at Cameron), and providing visiting fans with tickets isn't high priority. Speaking of tickets, I bought mine off StubHub. Tricia still does not know how much I paid, and I wouldn't dare put it here. But let's just say it will be the most I will ever pay to attend a sporting event.

The Crazies, already loud, took it up a notch as they were let inside, four or five students at a time. They shouted and jumped down the sidewalk, high-fiving alumni, making their way to the student section. By the time I got inside, thirty minutes later, three-quarters of the lower seats were packed, shoulder to shoulder, with body-painted maniacs chanting, "Let's go, Duke!"

Pregame at Cameron is a blur of noise and motion. My favorite moment was when the Duke pep band began to play Cee Lo Green's ode to the F-word, apparently assuming that the students wouldn't take this advantage to sing their feelings toward the UNC players warming up. They did, and a frantic band director waved his arms like a mad man, cutting the song off early.

I walked through the bowels of the arena. Narrow brick hallways and windows looking out into the dark night gave me the feeling I was in an old high school gymnasium. I took some stairs down a level and found myself courtside, standing next to Tim Brando. I probably could have wedged myself into the graduate student section, but I figured I already had an excellent seat. When you pay what I did, you expect a seat on the bench next to Coach K and, if the game gets out of hand, the opportunity to design an inbound play. I was wrong.

My seat was in the corner, in the top row. This wasn't a major issue, since the top row at Cameron would be about halfway up anywhere else. The problem was, when people on the next-to-last row sat down, I couldn't see anything except the back of their heads. I realized why there had been a plastic crate in my seat. I grabbed the crate, which I'd set behind my row, and put it on my seat. With my extra fifteen inches I could easily see over the heads below, but now I couldn't see the basket on the opposite end of the court because of the low roofline. However when I hunched over just enough, I found the sweet spot between the heads and the roof. And this is how I watched Duke and North Carolina play basketball for the 333rd time. You have no idea how much my neck hurt the next morning.

~~~

"For North Carolina, starting at guard, number five, Kendall Marshall."

The Cameron Crazies waved in unison at Kendall, as if they were actually being introduced, then chanted, "Hey Kendall … you suck!"

Somewhere a drum beat slowly, and with each beat the Crazies jumped. The drumbeat grew faster, and the jumps closer together, until the entire lower level of Cameron Indoor Stadium was a bouncing mass. The referee tossed the ball into the air, and it was on.

At least for UNC. The Tar Heels scored eight points before

Duke realized the game had begun. The Blue Devils eventually scored, but by then Carolina was off and running. On every trip down, someone in light blue was making a layup. The Tar Heels appeared to be the superior physical team. I wondered how or if Duke would get in the game. Maybe I'd get to hear the Cameron Crazies' famous cheer for when Duke is losing: "That's alright, that's okay, we're going to be your boss someday." Maybe the reason people hate Duke isn't so mysterious after all.

The Tar Heels, led by Tyler Zeller and John Henson, led Duke by as many as sixteen and took a fourteen-point lead to the locker room at halftime. Afterward Coach K attributed the poor start to his team being too excited. *Nuts* is the word he used, but how a team could play in that atmosphere and not be too excited is beyond me.

I stood up and tried to stretch, but my back was permanently hunched. I thought if nothing else I could live in the Duke Chapel and become Durham's Quasimodo.

The second half started, and Seth Curry, younger brother of Steph Curry, decided to singlehandedly keep the Blue Devils in the game. Curry poured in fourteen points in the first ten minutes of the second half, and improbably the Tar Heels' lead was gone. The game was tied at 54.

The Tar Heels made a single free throw on their next possession, regaining the lead by one, but when Duke's Ryan Kelly hit a three on the next possession, he gave the Blue Devils a lead they would not relinquish. From there it was the Nolan Smith show. Duke's senior guard scored twelve of his game-high thirty-four points in the final eight minutes, including the exclamation point, a tomahawk dunk in the game's final seconds.

After the game I walked back down to courtside and tried to soak it all in one last time. I don't have a bucket list of sporting events I have to see before I die, but I'm glad I saw this. If you ever get the chance, go. Just don't tell your wife how much the ticket cost.

Leaving Cameron, I followed the Crazies through a maze of gothic buildings back to the west quad, and soon the night was aglow with flames from the benches the Duke students were burning in celebration of a win over their archrival. The benches appeared to be homemade and designed specifically for burning. I'm not sure what would become of them had Carolina won, because they didn't look particularly comfortable for sitting. But I'm not sure that ever crossed the Crazies' minds. Even the Devils have to have a little faith.

~~~

The next morning Chapel Hill was covered in snow. Mitch was getting ready to go to his office, and we talked briefly about the game. He was encouraged by the Tar Heels' play, and with good reason. UNC beat Duke soundly a month later in the Dean Dome to win the ACC championship. Duke beat UNC a week after that to win the ACC tournament, and both teams advanced, as always, to the NCAA tournament, where the Devils fell to Arizona in the Sweet Sixteen, and the Tar Heels lost to Kentucky in the Elite Eight. I'm not exactly sure who has bragging rights after a season like that, but either way it was another terrific year of hoops on Tobacco Road.

Celtic F.C.
vs.
Rangers F.C.

Celtic Park – Glasgow, Scotland
February 20, 2011

We have just enough religion to make us hate,
but not enough to make us love one another.
—Jonathan Swift

A few years ago I decided to lend my allegiances to a European soccer club. I browsed the Internet, reading about teams on ESPN and Wikipedia, watched YouTube clips of famous games and goals, and decided I would root for Celtic F.C. out of the Scottish Premier League. I based this decision on the undeniable fact that Celtic, while not a European powerhouse, has cool uniforms.

I'm sorry, *kits*. They have really cool kits. That's what they call uniforms over there, the same way they call soccer "football," and the same way they call beans and tomatoes "breakfast." However for the benefit of my predominately American audience, I'm going to stick with the terms we use.[1]

Now I had a team, but my team was never on any of my three hundred cable channels until October 2008, when seemingly out of nowhere, Celtic was scheduled to play Manchester United on ESPN. I was beside myself. I set my DVR—the game would be played while I was at work—and bought a four-pack of Guinness, because this, I figured, is what soccer fans did.

Then Tricia and I sat down for an evening of soccer and beer.

---

1. USA! USA! USA!

My first taste of Guinness nearly killed me, and Tricia refused even a sip. Manchester United scored three goals, and Celtic scored none—the American football equivalent of a 35–0 beat down—and with that my interest began to wane.

It waned further the following May, when Kevin McDaid, a community worker in Northern Ireland, was beaten to death by a mob of forty youths. The mob was apparently celebrating Rangers' win over Dundee United, which gave them the Scottish Premier League championship over Celtic. That's when I realized I'd unwittingly chosen sides in perhaps the most violent rivalry in sports: Celtic vs. Rangers. I hid my recently purchased Celtic T-shirt in the bottom of my closet, in case a sectarian mob happened to wander through east-central Alabama.

~~~

The rivalry began in 1888, the same year Brother Walfrid, an Irish missionary priest, founded Celtic Football Club as a Catholic charity. Celtic's first match was against Rangers, a 5–2 win, and I doubt any in attendance would have believed it to be the first of 395 matches to date.

To explain the intricacies of a rivalry this complex, I'd need more than the handful of paragraphs I have here. So I'll have to tell a simplified Celtic–Rangers story using broad generalizations that certainly do not apply to everyone involved, but you'll get the idea.

In 1845 the Great Famine hit Ireland, killing over one million people and bringing with it disease and mass starvation. During this time a large number of Irish, most of them poor and Catholic, immigrated to Glasgow for work, where the local Protestants, who feared they might lose their jobs, didn't embrace them.

In this hostile environment, Brother Walfrid founded Celtic in part to raise money for his charity, The Poor Children's Dinner Table. Walfrid's soup kitchen was a response to Protestant missionaries' using their own soup kitchens to evangelize Catholic youths. But Walfrid wanted Celtic to play great soccer too, in hopes they could erase the myth of Catholic inferiority. As Franklin Foer puts it, Celtic–Rangers "is an unfinished fight over the Protestant Reformation."

With Celtic winning titles—four league championships in their first six seasons—conservative, middle-class Protestant Glaswegians wanted a team of their own, and soon they latched on to Rangers, giving the team an identity they still carry.

Violence was present from the beginning. A 1909 Scottish Cup final holds the somewhat dubious distinction of hosting the first soccer riot. Fans set the stadium on fire, and when the firemen came to douse the blaze, the rioters threw rocks at them.

The sectarian violence associated with the Old Firm, as the rivalry is called, did not hurt the teams. Supporters identified so strongly that attendance soared, turning both teams into financial juggernauts and sending them into the stratosphere of Scottish soccer. Going into this season, either Rangers or Celtic had won 95 of the 114 league championships. Brian Phillips wrote for *Slate*, "If either club hadn't existed, the other would likely have lived out its years quietly—nothing more than a run-of-the-mill, non-politically signifying soccer club."

But both clubs exist, and it's no wonder Irish Catholic, working-class Celtic and Protestant, middle-class Rangers began to symbolize more than soccer clubs to both sides of The Troubles in Northern Ireland. Celtic fans sing songs in praise of the IRA, while Rangers sing about the UDA, a Protestant paramilitary group.

The Old Firm brings together political strife, religious conflict, class warfare, and fierce nationalism. Add to all of this the fact that Rangers and Celtic are the two great soccer clubs in Scotland, and thus generally wouldn't like each other much anyway. It's really no wonder the rivalry produces such violence.

According to a group that monitors such things, on Old Firm weekends, admissions in Glasgow's emergency rooms increase nine-fold. Domestic violence rises 41 percent on days when Celtic and Rangers play. In just the last decade there have been numerous deaths associated with the Old Firm, and once a Celtic fan was shot in the chest with a crossbow while leaving a pub.[2] This is why I had to see it myself.

~~~

I've known Jordan Ross for a long time. He is the younger cousin of a college friend, and we began sneaking him into the Auburn student section for football games when he was in the eighth grade. Now a graduate student at Auburn, Jordan has been sitting in that student section for most of his life, but he is also a soccer fanatic. So when I mentioned a free trip to Scotland to watch an Old Firm match, he didn't hesitate.

We flew out of Atlanta on Wednesday, February 16. Just before boarding I got a text message informing me someone had poisoned the two oak trees that make up Toomer's Corner in Auburn. The trees were not expected to live, and I was sick. I began to fear that the Auburn–Alabama rivalry had gone too far and was turning people into morons. I doubted Scotland could ever match the insanity I was leaving at home.

Jordan and I landed at London's Gatwick Airport around 7:00 a.m. local time. After a quick breakfast, we boarded a train for central London. Tricia and I had been there the previous summer, and it felt like a tourist destination. With the sun out, the parks and cathedrals full of people, it was easy to think everyone you saw was on *holiday*, sorry, vacation. But this morning was cold and cloudy, and we were on a train full of grumpy Brits obviously going to work. It was Thursday after all, and I began to feel we were intruding on their routine.

In London, we fought our way through Tube station after Tube station, eventually making our way to the Holiday Inn in Regents Park. The problem with European travel is you always seem to land early in the morning, but it still feels a little past

---

2. A freaking crossbow!

midnight. You are sleepy, but you cannot check into your room for another six or seven hours. We left our bags at the front desk and stumbled around London like zombies.

First up was Big Ben and Parliament, then a tour of Westminster Abbey, if only to get out of the cold. Three months later an important wedding would draw the eyes of the world, but this day it was just Jordan and me and a few off-season tourists. I realized many of the kings and queens buried under our feet were in a way responsible for the rivalry we'd soon witness.

We ate fish and chips at a pub near our hotel for dinner. Sure it was stereotypical, but it was also delicious. Then back at the hotel we had the dreamless sleep only jet lag produces.

The next morning we toured Emirates Stadium, home of Arsenal F.C., a popular team in the English Premier League. We told our guide we were headed to Glasgow to see the Old Firm match that weekend. He looked at us as if we'd said we were going to Tehran to put on a passion play.

After the tour, we tried to find White Hart Lane, home of another English team, Tottenham Hotspur, but realized we were lost in a rather dodgy part of London, and we were both thankful when we made it back to the relative safety of a Tube stop.[3] Back at the hotel I called Tricia, who wasn't thrilled to be in Auburn working, to tell her about our day.

"Are you guys going to get tea for two today?" she asked, after listening to me drone on about the stadium tour.

"Uh," I said. "I don't think so."

"Why not?" Tricia demanded. "You certainly enjoyed it last summer."

"Isn't it kind of weird for two guys to have tea together?"

"No weirder than two guys going to Europe together."

Touché.

After an evening of shopping at Piccadilly Circus, where

---

3. A few months later London was engulfed in riots. Anyone want to guess where they began? That's right, Tottenham.

Jordan bought more soccer paraphernalia than we'd be able to haul home, we watched a few hours' worth of peculiar British dating shows back at the hotel. The next morning we headed to Glasgow by train.

As the train wound into northern England and eventually Scotland, we began to see more and more snow on the hills. Field after field flew past, rock walls marking their boundaries, sheep eating their grass, broken up by nameless towns that I will likely never see again, church towers dotting the skylines. It really was a lovely four hours, except for the two kids in front of me who didn't know how to silence their video games.

I'd checked the map a dozen times, but walking out of Glasgow's Central Station I still felt lost. After reading the street signs on a couple of corners—a sure sign you're a tourist—we had our bearings and began the eight-block walk to our hotel.

Rick Steves, in his guide to the UK I read before the trip, advises not to go near the Clyde River, because it is "nothing but thugs and prostitutes." This, of course, is exactly where our hotel was located. It was nice enough though, and after checking in we explored Glasgow.

Glasgow is not a beautiful city, at least not in the way normal people use the word *beautiful*. It is, however, old and has interesting architecture, so even though we were walking through a Scottish version of Birmingham, Alabama, it felt exotic.

We walked up and down Argyle and Buchanan Streets, Jordan resisted the urge to go in the soccer shops, and eventually we made our way to George's Square, where we took awkward photos of each other. Because it felt like a vacation, we felt we should be out enjoying ourselves. But it was freezing, so we headed to the hotel to catch a couple dating shows before dinner instead.

Finding tickets to see the Old Firm match was interesting. I couldn't find a European equivalent to StubHub, and the online brokers I did find seemed to think £425[4] was a reasonable price

---

4. Roughly 4.5 million American dollars.

for a seat. I logged on to Talk Celtic, a Celtic message board, and asked the members for some advice. The guys were friendly—they all called me "mate"—and pointed out that only a very wealthy moron would pay £425 for an Old Firm ticket. Turns out the club still had hospitality packages available for about $200 each. This got us not only a ticket but also a three-course meal at Celtic Park the night before the match. Around 6:00 p.m. we hailed a cab to Parkhead.

We were both nervous about the dinner. I pictured it as an IRA initiation, where Jordan and I would be asked to bomb a unionist pub. But when we walked into the restaurant overlooking Celtic Park, it looked like a wedding reception. Relieved, we found our seats.

They placed us at a table with a father and son from Australia. The son worked in London, and his dad was visiting. As the dinner went on, it became obvious the son had just discovered Illuminati videos on YouTube. He spent most of the evening trying to convince us everything was a conspiracy.

Soon an older couple from Ireland joined our table. The man was quiet, his wife quieter, and the six of us sat at times in awkward silence. When the Irishman did speak, Jordan and I found him nearly impossible to understand. Fortunately, the Australian father could understand us both and translated our various forms of English around the table.

Lentil soup was followed by roast sirloin, grilled salmon, and a hodgepodge of vegetables. "What is this?" I asked, pointing to a brown glob on my plate that appeared to have little seeds inside it.

"Ates aggis," said the Irishman.

I looked to the Australian for a translation.

"It's haggis," he said.

"Okay, but what is it?" I repeated.

"Just try it," they told me, so I did. I thought it was a little too spicy, but generally tasty, so I ate the whole blob. After dessert they told me haggis consists of the heart, liver, and lungs of a sheep. Bon appétit.

After dinner the crowd of mostly out-of-towners was addressed by two Celtic legends, George McCluskey and Joe McBride. At least I assumed they were legends; they could have pulled two men off the street and told me they played for Celtic in the sixties and I would have been none the wiser. Together, Jordan and I probably comprehended about 8 percent of what was said during the question and answer period, although we deduced both men predicted a Celtic win on Sunday.

~~~

The next morning we had breakfast at the hotel. Haggis was once again on the menu, but this time I passed.[5] The game started at noon, and there was a line for cabs at our hotel, so we walked downtown, thinking it would be quicker, but all we found was an endless line of Celtic fans waiting for cabs of their own. We watched the line move slowly and calculated that if we waited here we would certainly miss the game, and likely our flight the next morning. We ran back to the hotel and joined its now much longer line.

I panicked. When you fly four thousand miles for the sole purpose of watching a soccer match, you'd rather not miss the soccer match. At the front of the queue, sorry, line, four women dressed head to toe in Celtic gear were getting in a large cab. One of them made eye contact with Jordan in his Celtic scarf and said, "You lads going to Parkhead?" We both nodded, and she waved us over.

"Is this is a good idea?" Jordan whispered as we walked toward the cab.

"No," I replied.

The ladies were from Belfast, Ireland, all Celtic fans, and all, best I could tell, crazy. Within seconds they realized we were

---

5. I don't know what it is about the UK and breakfast, but someone needs to introduce these folks to my two best friends, Cap'n Crunch and Count Chocula.

from the States and began the Irish inquisition: "Big Hoops fans from the States, eh?"[6]

"Not really," I explained. "I'm a writer, and I'm writing a book on sports rivalries."

"If you're the writer, then who is this?" one of them asked, grabbing Jordan's coat sleeve.

"That's my friend Jordan. He's a big soccer fan, so I thought he'd be helpful to bring along."

"So Chad the writer and Jordan his assistant. What part of the States are you boys from?"

"Alabama," we said in unison.

"Alabama," they all repeated in unison, mocking our accents. "Know Forrest Gump now, do ya?"

At this they apologized, figuring it was as annoying as people from the States asking them if they knew leprechauns.

This was their third trip to see Celtic play, the home team losing in their first two visits. I asked if they were friends with any Rangers fans back home, and one of the girls said her friend and co-worker was a massive Rangers fan. "And you guys get along fine?" I asked.

"Sure," she said. "Although when I told him I was coming here for the weekend he told me he hopes I get my throat slit."

With friends like that, who needs enemies?

~~~

Two weeks after my trip to Glasgow, Scottish columnist Alan Cochrane called the Old Firm "a depressing curse on the face of Scotland." But these four Irish gals didn't seem that bad. They gave us gum, for crying out loud. In fact, every fan I spoke to seemed to abhor the violence and bigotry surrounding the Old Firm just as much as Alan Cochrane does.

Neil, a Rangers fan who incidentally is married to a Catholic, Celtic supporter, told me, "The bigotry and violence is the worst

6. Celtic is sometimes called the Hoops because their jerseys consist of green and white horizontal stripes, which I guess look like hoops. They are also sometimes called the Bhoys, but I do not know why.

part of the rivalry."

Martin McGowan, a Celtic supporter from Glasgow, echoed Neil's sentiments. "The worst thing about the rivalry is the hatred, mindless violence, bigotry, sectarianism, and ignorance. Someone will want to fight you just for the colors you are wearing, and there are certain parts of the city you can't even go to."

Even the stereotypes began to break down as I spoke to fans. When I asked them to describe fans of their rival team—a loaded question if there ever was one—both Carol, a Rangers supporter from Edinburgh, and Andy, a Celtic fan from Glasgow, told me, "There's no real difference, we're just Scots who cheer for different teams."

Wait, what? What about the whole Protestant–Catholic thing people get shot with crossbows over? Then I realized fans on both sides were prefacing answers to my more spiritual questions with "I don't believe in God" or "I'm not really a person of faith."

As a respondent told the Glasgow City Council during its research on sectarianism in the city, "It has nothing to do with Catholics and Protestants, it's the new religions of Celtic and Rangers."

Franklin Foer talked about this in his brilliant book, *How Soccer Explains the World*. Foer says that while discrimination has faded, "the city has kept alive its soccer tribalism, despite the logic of history, because it provides the city with a kind of pornographic pleasure."

Rangers fans singing about being "up to their knees in Fenian blood" don't literally want to be up to their knees in Fenian blood, the same way Duke fans don't literally want UNC fans to go to hell. I once saw an Ole Miss fan scream at an injured LSU player—in front of her two children—that she hoped his neck was broken. It is a pornographic pleasure to stir up this sort of hatred, and I'm afraid we've all done it on some level.

A Rangers spokesman once famously used the phrase

"ninety-minute bigots" to explain the apparent religious hatred amongst Old Firm fans. This may be true, but for everyone I spoke to who despised the violence, I talked to someone else who'd experienced it outside of a game.

"I was assaulted by a group of Rangers fans on Christmas."

"I was spit on by Celtic fans while walking with my children."

"I was beat up by kids in school simply for being Catholic."

"I had a Celtic fan threaten to stab me."

If someone pulls a knife on you, or even spits on you, you don't forget it. In the world of sports, where my team is my identity, it's easy to place your feelings for those who have wronged you onto a rival fan base as a whole. Mix the hyper-emotional atmosphere of a rivalry game with just a touch of Scotch whiskey, and you have a recipe for violence.

It's a cycle. As one young Celtic fan told me, "I hate them because they hate us." As long as both teams are making fortunes partially on their image, it's hard to see an end in sight. Both clubs have campaigns aimed at ending sectarian violence, Celtic's Bhoys against Bigotry and Rangers' Follow with Pride, but it takes more than campaigns. Perhaps ejecting fans that sing offensive songs or waive bigoted banners.

This being said, an audit from the Crown Office in Edinburgh found that only a quarter of the religiously aggravated crimes in Glasgow had anything to do with football. Alan Cochrane is right that there is "a depressing curse on the face of Scotland." That curse isn't so much the sectarianism that exists during the ninety minutes Celtic and Rangers are playing, it's the sectarianism that still exists when they are not.

~~~

The cabbie dropped us off as close to Celtic Park as he could. The girls paid for the cab, gave us both hugs, and disappeared into the river of green and white flowing toward the stadium.

The police put on quite a show of force; dozens of them in

full riot gear circled the stadium on horseback and made me nervous. People sang songs with their thick accents, and I only occasionally recognized a word, most of them unprintable. I expected to see fights before the game and figured I might even try to shove Jordan into one, but I didn't see a single Rangers fan before the game. Later I learned why.

Entering the stadium was a little different. First the police pat down, which I expected in a rivalry like this. Then you scan your ticket against a screen on the wall, and when the light turns green, you are ushered, one at a time, through a full body turnstile that looks like it might chop you into tiny pieces. We made it through safely and joined the mass of green climbing to the upper level. Just as we found our seats, high in the Lisbon Lions Stand, the loudspeakers began to play "You'll Never Walk Alone."

"You'll Never Walk Alone"[7] is a Rodgers and Hammerstein show tune from the 1940s musical *Carousel* and not typically the kind of song you hear at sporting events. But Celtic have adopted it as their pre-match anthem and sing it in full-voice as the Bhoys wait to take the pitch. You can watch a video of it on my website. It still gives me goose bumps, so I cannot imagine what it feels like for the players in the tunnel.

The teams took the pitch, and I finally noticed the Rangers fans. They were occupying the corner sections on the lower level and a couple of sections above those in the upper deck. College football fans are familiar with this setup, but at Auburn, while the visitors have a defined section, there are usually pockets of visiting fans spread throughout the stadium. Here, the sections on either side of the Rangers fans were left empty, and in each row of those empty sections stood two serious looking policemen. There was not a single Rangers fan sitting among the Celtic faithful, unless they were in disguise.

7. Perhaps more famously than Celtic, Liverpool F.C. of the English Premier League also sings "You'll Never Walk Alone" pre-match. Which club began the tradition is often debated on the Internet, but I've learned my lesson about picking sides.

This made me nervous for the Rangers fans, but they were loud, decked out in their royal blue, with a few in King Billy's orange.[8] Best I could tell, they were not intimidated at all. As if to prove this point, pre-match they held aloft a huge banner that read "Where e'er we go, we fear no foe."

The match began sloppily. This is pretty universal in rivalry games. The atmosphere and nerves are a little too much for most players. Of course, I knew it was sloppy only because Jordan told me.

Sixteen minutes in, Chris Commons found Celtic's best player, Gary Hooper, at the top of the penalty box. Celtic are sometimes called the Hoops, and they were founded in 1888, so for their best player to wear #88 and be named Hooper is like the Yankees' best player being named Pinstripe. Hooper took the pass between two defenders, and with a quick poke of the ball he was by them, only the goalie between him and ecstasy. The stadium took a collective breath, and Hooper struck from six yards out, through the goalie's legs, into the back of the net. Parkhead went mad. Jordan and I were on our feet before we realized it, hugging Scottish strangers and singing Depeche Mode's "I Just Can't Get Enough."[9]

Ten minutes later Georgios Samaras hit Emilio Izaguirre on a long pass up the left side. Gary Hooper sprinted like a mad man behind the play, and from our seats high above the pitch we could see it all develop. Izaguirre skipped a pass all the way across the penalty area, catching the tip end of Gary Hooper's sliding foot. The celebration began before the ball even crossed the goal line. Fans danced in the aisles, making noise like I'd never heard before. The man behind us, who we'd met pre-match, now insisted Jordan and I buy season tickets and move to

---

8. Rangers' colors are blue and red, but sometimes you'll see their fans in orange to commemorate King William III, aka William of Orange, who ejected the Catholic monarchy in 1688. This only helps endear them more to Celtic supporters.

9. I don't know why, but this is the song they play whenever they score a goal, and at times the crowd will just start singing it, even the synthesizer part of the chorus.

Glasgow.

For the rest of the half, Celtic fans sang songs, but neither Jordan nor I could make out the lyrics. Perhaps they sang about the IRA, or maybe they sang more from the Depeche Mode catalog, I could not tell you. At halftime, huge banners were unfurled and passed around the stadium, one a massive Irish flag.

The second half began, and nothing much was happening. A 2–0 lead in soccer is not insurmountable, but it can feel like it. Even so, the crowd was wild as ever, even the Rangers fans, who continued to cheer on their team in full voice. Finally, in the sixty-ninth minute, Chris Commons took the ball about twenty yards out, left his defender, and uncorked a wicked shot that sent the Rangers goalie to his right while the ball spun back left into the net. Three–nil, and the earth shook.

The last twenty minutes of the match were basically a party. The crowd sang, "Can you hear the Rangers sing? Nooooo, nooooo," and chanted, "We can see you sneakin' out," to the Rangers fans who decided 3–0 was plenty of soccer for one day. Before either Jordan or I realized it, the men on either side of us, men you wouldn't want to meet in a dark alley, put their arms around us and began jumping up and down with the rest of the stadium, singing, "Let's all do the huddle, let's all do the huddle, ah ahhhhh ah ah, ah ahhhhh ah ah." It was the craziest sporting event I've ever attended.

All too soon the game was over. The Celtic players stood and applauded their fans, who stood and applauded them back, then we all filed out into the cloudy Glasgow afternoon. We were told at the hotel that walking back was our only option, despite the three mile distance; it appeared everyone else was doing just that, so we joined the pilgrimage. We walked down Gallowgate, toward the city center, passing bar after bar with green and orange facades and Irish flags waving out front. At each bar, we lost more and more of the Celtic fans, until only a handful were left as we arrived downtown. Jordan and I stopped at a soccer shop and got strange looks for buying both Celtic and Rangers souvenirs. Then it was back to the hotel for a few more dating shows and some room service haggis.

The following morning, we left Glasgow and had a six-hour layover in Amsterdam—enough time to explore the Venice of the north, assuming we didn't board the wrong train and spend an hour traveling into the Dutch wilderness. But that is another story for another book, I suppose.

~~~

In the end, Rangers won the Scottish Premier League championship on the final day, by one point, over Celtic. I'd like to report that the season passed without incident, and the violence associated with this incredible rivalry is a thing of the past, but that would be a lie. A month after our trip, Celtic manager Neil Lennon received a parcel bomb. The package was not opened, but authorities say the bomb was powerful enough to have killed Lennon. Weeks later a crazed fan ran onto the pitch and attacked Lennon. Even the match we attended had 229 arrests. Of course 229 people out of 60,000 is a small percentage, but if one of those small percentage spits on you or shoots a crossbow at you, it's easier for you to hate everyone who wears their colors, not just those who take things too far and ruin sports for everyone.

I thought about this game and this rivalry a lot during the year, when people insisted the Alabama–Auburn rivalry had gotten out of hand. I've seen out of hand. We're not even close.

Yankees vs. Red Sox

Fenway Park – Boston, Massachusetts
April 8, 2011

Hating the New York Yankees is as American as pizza pie, unwed mothers, and cheating on your income tax.
—Mike Royko

I slept through September 11. No, not the entire day, but when I woke up for my 1:00 p.m. class all four planes had crashed, and both towers had fallen. By this time ABC News had commandeered ESPN, and the first image I saw on TV was the New York City skyline covered by the debris cloud, with the headline "America under Attack." A child of the eighties, my first thought was that the Soviet Union had reformed overnight and launched a nuclear barrage on my homeland. Looking back, I'm not sure which is scarier, the Soviets—who had enough nuclear weapons to destroy the earth and every other planet in our solar system, but who were apparently so unconvinced by their own ideology that they switched sides during a fifteen-round boxing match[1] —or the extremists, who don't have nuclear weapons but believe so fervently in their cause that they will die, just so I will live in terror.

It bothers me to think someone hates me. I know that's the most self-centered way to think about 9/11, but I imagine it bothers others as well. Knowing there are men who would rather

1. Yo Adrian!

slit my throat than shake my hand, even if I sent them an edible arrangement, it's disconcerting. I'm a nice guy. I have like 1,500 Facebook friends. But these people seem unflinching in their hate, so even though I shouldn't, I kind of hate them back.

Hate can control us, turn us into people we are not, and make us do things we would never do otherwise. And it was in those terror-filled, hate mongering weeks after 9/11 that I did something I thought I would never do. I cheered for the New York Yankees.

~~~

In the 1955 Broadway musical *Damn Yankees*, middle-aged realtor Joe Boyd sells his soul to the Devil himself. In return, Boyd's favorite team, the lowly Washington Senators, will finally beat those damn Yankees. Hatred for a team manifests in many ways, although rarely in the form of musical theatre. But *Damn Yankees* won the Tony for best musical and had a very successful run on Broadway. This leads me to believe there are lots of people out there, even in the musical theatre community, who relate to a man willing to spend eternity in hellfire just so his team will finally beat the New York Yankees.

Once again I turned to my social network to tell me, in 140 characters or less, why they hate the Yankees. A couple of folks said the Yankees represent everything that is wrong in the world, which seems a bit of a stretch. My friend Knox McCoy said hating the Yankees is in our DNA, and anyone who likes them is obviously a mutant. One friend said he didn't hate the Yankees, but they weren't in his top 29 favorite major league teams either. Another said, "I hate them like Glenn Beck hates Obama. I regret their existence, but their existence does give me something to do, namely, hate them." Yet another said he simply hates baseball, and since the Yanks epitomize baseball, he hates them. Fair enough, but the vast majority said they hate the Yankees because of Yankees fans.

Again, for the most part my Internet friends are southerners;

I don't think many actually come into regular contact with Yankees fans. Perhaps it's just the name "Yankees" and unresolved Civil War issues going on here. But Yankees hate is certainly not limited to the former Confederate States.

My friend Matt lives in Grand Rapids, Michigan, and is a huge Detroit Tigers fan. In 2006, the Tigers defeated the Yankees in the American League Division Series. Matt was at game four in Detroit and saw his Tigers knock the Bronx Bombers out of the playoffs.

"Here I was at the game," said Matt. "My team just did what very few thought possible. For the first time in my life as a fan my beloved baseball team won a playoff series. I should be thrilled, and I am, but what's the first thing I do after the final out is recorded? Hug my friend in the seat next to me? High-five all the random strangers in front and behind me? Nope. I yell out some not-so-kind comments and flip the bird at the Yankees players as they slowly walk off the field. Here I am, at what is truthfully the best moment of fandom in my life, and rather than be totally happy for my team, I'm showing the other team how much I dislike them and how happy I am at their failure."

Matt's story is slightly disturbing, but I bet more than one of you can relate. Germans have a word for deriving pleasure from others' misfortune: *schadenfreude*. But this is more than someone's misfortune; it's your enemy's misfortune. An enemy that not only you hate, but all of baseball hates. A team people who don't even care about baseball hate. A team *GQ* once called "Satan's chosen team."

Mike, a Sox fan in Braintree, Massachusetts, told me, "Sure, I hate them, and I love it when they lose. But then I read Proverbs 24:17–18, and I don't know how to feel."

Not having every verse of the Bible memorized, I had to ask, "What does Proverbs 24:17–18 say?"

"It says, 'Do not gloat when your enemy falls; when they stumble, do not let your heart rejoice, or the Lord will see and disapprove and turn his wrath away from them.' And when I read that I don't know how to act when the Yankees lose, because if I enjoy it too much, God might make them start winning."

You see, *this* is what the Yankees do to people.

~~~

I was raised on baseball. Apart from one ill-fated season of junior high football, baseball was the only sport I played growing up. I usually played first base, not because I was any good at it, but because I was a big kid and made a good target for the other infielders to throw at. I stopped playing after ninth grade, in part because I couldn't hit a curve ball,[2] but mostly because I'd just achieved my most memorable sports moment—throwing a ball from left field over the third base dugout and striking our second basemen's mother in the neck—and I figured there was nothing left to accomplish.

In the summers, when I wasn't playing baseball, I spent countless evenings watching the Atlanta Braves lose in every way imaginable. In the South, kids in the eighties grew up on Dale Murphy, Glenn Hubbard, and Bob Horner in those baby blue uniforms. Put two or more southern men of a certain age in a room, and they can spend hours naming old Braves players, giving nods to the more obscure ones like Paul Assenmacher or Oddibe McDowell.

We watched the games with our dads because baseball is a father–son sport. It was a decade of terrible baseball, and we all suffered psychological damage from hearing "mathematical elimination" too often, but we never minded bad baseball as long as we watched it with our dads. And even if we rebelled and refused to watch, we knew ghosts in our cornfields would help us relive it years later.

So it was no surprise that when I asked my dad which trip he'd like to accompany me on, he chose Yankees vs. Red Sox at Fenway Park. It's the greatest rivalry in baseball, perhaps the

---

2. Or a fastball, or a change up, or a slider, or an underhand toss.

greatest rivalry in sports, played at the most famous ballpark in the country. It's baseball. It's fathers and sons.

I checked the Red Sox's schedule to see when the Bronx Bombers would first visit, and to my delight, saw the Yankees were slotted for the home opener in April. It was perfect: opening day at Fenway Park with my dad. Of course I didn't know then the Sox would be 0–6 going into the opener, but hey, you can't have everything.

~~~

I doubt I will ever fly without thinking about 9/11. Not in a paralyzing, get-me-off-this-plane-that-man-looks-like-a-terrorist sort of way, but just a low-grade uneasiness as I go through the security line in my socks. Dad and I boarded in Atlanta around noon on Thursday, April 7, and we were Boston bound. I'm hyper-observant on planes, another post-9/11 symptom, and noticed the man in front of me reading a book about the 9/11 hijackers. I wondered if a less enjoyable book to read on a plane exists,[3] then remembered the books I'd brought were titled *A Long Way Down* and *Now I Can Die Happy*. I prayed this wasn't a sign.

We landed without incident at Logan International Airport in Boston, then took a cab to our hotel which, despite what Priceline thought, was nowhere near the airport. The Red Sox had recently lost their sixth game of the season, and our cab driver, a man who appeared to be no stranger to knife fights, wasn't hopeful for a miraculous turnaround. "The bums are going to lose 162 games," he growled, while driving like a stunt man in a Vin Diesel film.

"They'll turn it around. They've got too much talent," I said, trying to cheer up the man who seemed determined to end our lives in a fiery crash.

"Oh and one-sixty-two. You just watch!"

The more he thought about the Red Sox, the worse his driv-

---

3. Perhaps *History of Aviation Disasters*, Vol. 1.

ing became, so I agreed to disagree so long as he got us to the hotel alive.

After checking in, I called my friend Bryan Allain. Bryan is a humor blogger (*bryanallain.com*) who lives in Intercourse, Pennsylvania.[4] He is also the biggest Red Sox fan I know. I figured if I wanted to truly experience Fenway, I needed to experience it with a zealot.

Bryan was staying in town with his brother, Jordan, and they picked us up in Bryan's minivan. From there I don't know exactly what happened, because Dad and I both covered our eyes as Bryan swerved, one-handed, through Boston traffic, using the other hand to navigate with his iPhone. We arrived, by the grace of God, at a place called The Barking Crab.

The restaurant sits on Boston Harbor, close to where the Boston Tea Party took place. Bryan wedged his van into a parking spot, and the four of us went inside.

Fighting the urge to order ten pounds of Maine lobster for $289, I ordered clam chowder and crab cakes. Dad, who doesn't hear well, told the waitress he'd have whatever I ordered. Bryan ordered the chowder as well, but I noticed that after being back in Boston for only a few hours he pronounced it "chowdah."

Some may think I am making a big deal out of nothing, that this hate in sports, or whatever you want to call it, isn't worth worrying about. But when I talk to fans like Bryan, fans who live daily inside one of the most intense rivalries in sports, I know I'm not just making this up.

"My son, Parker, was four when he met his first Yankees fan," Bryan said. "It was my friend Dan, and when he told Parker, 'I don't like the Red Sox, I like the Yankees,' I thought Parker's head was going to explode. I could see the gears turning in his pint-sized head. 'Why would anyone like the Yankees, and why would my dad be friends with anyone who likes the Yankees?' He had the same look of fear and confusion on his face

---

4. Must. Resist. Joke.

that he had when he saw alligators at SeaWorld a few months earlier."

"Wait, Parker had the same reaction when he met a Yankees fan as he did when he saw an alligator? Had you been telling him that Yankees fans eat people?"

"Maybe."

When we talked about the hatred of our rivals in light of our beliefs, Bryan said, "I don't think Jesus could have picked three more challenging words to stick back-to-back than 'love your enemies.'"

"What about 'tickle your enemies'?"

"That would be pretty challenging too, but I think loving them is harder. Not, 'hey, try your best not to hate your enemies,' but, 'love your enemies.'"

I asked Bryan if he thought Jesus had sports fans in mind when he spoke about loving our enemies.

"No, but the thing is, if I can't love fans of my rival team, how am I going to be able to love enemies who actually want to do me harm?"

Even though Bryan and I are about the same age, he has a 2–0 lead on me in the procreation department, and like most of my friends who are parents, Bryan seems to learn as many life lessons from raising his children as his children learn from him.

"In Parker's first year of t-ball we were having Sunday dinner at my in-laws, when my sister-in-law mentioned she'd heard all the kids would be divided up randomly onto four teams, and she'd heard one of the teams would be called the Yankees. So there was a 25 percent chance Parker would be a Yankee, and to me those odds weren't just terrifying, they were completely unacceptable. A few weeks later I was telling an old college friend about all of this, laying out my reasons for being enraged, when my friend said, 'Wow, no idolatry happening there at all.' I try to teach my kids lessons with sports, and I think that's when I realized I was being taught a lesson myself."

I tried not to think how I will act when my future son is drafted to play t-ball for a team called the Crimson Tide.

"Hatred is hatred," Bryan told me. "Whether it's directed at a person who commits terrible acts of injustice against innocents, or if it's directed at someone wearing a Yankees hat."

Then he said something very interesting: "I've found most people feel more intense dislike for teams they hate than they do for things in the world that might actually deserve their disdain. Think about it, if I tell a Broncos fan about some injustice going on in Africa, it might disturb them for a bit, but if I start making them watch highlights of the Raiders beating Denver, they'll be angrier than Africanized bees. I'd be the same way if you showed me the Bucky Dent homerun over and over, and that shouldn't sit well with us.

"So I've tried to raise Parker, and my daughter Kylie, to not hate the Yankees. I encourage them to cheer for the Sox, and root against New York. And I tell them it's okay to revel in a New York loss as much as it is to revel in a Boston win. But we don't hate the Yankees as a team, and we don't hate their players, and we don't hate their fans. I think it's more than just semantics. It's a mindset. I know Parker has a long way to go before he can understand how difficult it is to love his enemies. Honestly I've got a long way to go too, we all do. But it's not a concept we master all at once. It's something we engrain into our lives little by little, with God's help."

~~~

The next morning Dad and I boarded the hotel shuttle to the closest T Station. The shuttle driver, like our cabbie, was convinced the Red Sox would make baseball history by losing all 162 games this season. I let this poor guy wallow in his misery.

We spent most of the overcast morning walking around the harbor; Dad took photographs, and I wished I'd packed warmer clothes. Around eleven we warmed up at Dunkin' Donuts, then took the Green Line to Fenway Park.

At each stop our train picked up more and more Sox fans. When they all piled out at Kenmore, we kept our seats, unaware the Kenmore stop is actually closer to Fenway Park than the speciously named Fenway stop. It isn't *that* far out of the way though, and as we rounded the corner onto Brookline Avenue, we saw the massive CITGO sign towering in the distance, the same sign that has loomed over the Green Monster for decades. Bryan told me later that the elementary school rumor chain always had Boston's slugger du jour hitting the sign in batting practice. That the sign is roughly 1,200 feet from home plate and over a hundred feet off the ground never squashed this persistent rumor.

On the corner of Yawkey Way and Brookline, baseball's equivalent to the Pearly Gates, we both stood smiling. On game days, Yawkey Way is blocked off. You need a ticket to enter the land where beer and bratwursts flow, but we didn't want to go in yet, so we wandered.

Words don't capture the wonder of Fenway Park. Today stadiums are built in the suburbs, off the interstate, surrounded by sprawling parking lots. They are convenient and modern and soulless. Getting in and out of Fenway is a bit of a cluster, and some of the seats don't technically have a view of the field. Maybe I'm an old soul, but to see baseball at Fenway is to see it the way God, or at least Abner Doubleday, wanted you to see it.

Dad and I pushed our way through the crowds toward Lansdowne Street, the road running directly behind the Green Monster. We sat down to wait for Bryan, and just under three hours before the first pitch, we heard the first chant of "Yankees suck!"

You hear this a lot in Boston, always at Sox games, and occasionally during championship celebrations of teams in other sports, but the thing is, the Yankees don't really suck. Not at baseball. Perhaps they're poor drivers, or maybe not very good at water skiing, but no one who chants "Yankees suck" can truly believe they suck at baseball, unless the chanter sucks at baseball history.

Love Thy Rival

In 1919, the Red Sox were baseball royalty. Of the sixteen World Series, the Sox had won five, including four of the last eight. But Sox star player Babe Ruth (maybe you've heard of him) wanted more money, and Boston owner Harry Frazee didn't want to pay him. Frazee instead sold Ruth to the Yankees, who up until then had never played in a World Series. Over the next eighty-three seasons, the Yankees would play in thirty-nine World Series, winning twenty-six of them. The Red Sox would play in four, losing them all. This was the Curse of the Bambino.

The Red Sox finally won a World Series in 2004, breaking the curse, with a win again in 2007. But even if they win the next nineteen World Series, they will still trail the Yankees. The Yankees have as many World Series wins as twenty-one other major league teams combined. Their twenty-seven championships are nearly triple the St. Louis Cardinals', who have the second most with ten. Heck, the Yankees have lost more World Series, thirteen, than anyone else has won. Say what you want about the New York Yankees, but if you say they suck, don't do it with a straight face.

~~~

Bryan appeared, decked head to toe in Sox gear, and the three of us walked back to the Yawkey gate and went inside. Inside a souvenir shop, I contemplated buying a Red Sox cap, but the bandwagon potential is so high I passed.

I mentioned this to Bryan, and he said, "Cheering for the Red Sox has become a little too cool. We call it the pink hat issue because there are so many females wearing Sox gear. It's mildly annoying."

GQ jumped on this when ranking the worst sports fans in America. "They have the biggest legion of bandwagon fans in the country, pushing past the Pinstripes as baseball's top-drawing road team in 2005, 2007, and 2008. These days, Red Sox fans are indistinguishable from Yankees fans—just with more grating accents." Ouch.

Walt, a Yankees fan from Staten Island, brought this up when I asked him to describe a rival fan. "They love their team," he said. "I've got to give them that. But once they finally had success and could no longer identify with the losing tradition of the Red Sox of old, they became just like the hated Yankees. Buying players, bandwagon fans. They've become Yankees Jr. They've become everything they despised in us."

"We're the same," Regina, a Yankees fan from Chatham, told me, and in the context of this rivalry, it was probably the meanest thing she could say.

~~~

After a cart lunch of sausage dogs and bottled Coke, we walked inside the hallowed grounds. I never missed playing baseball after I hung up my glove in the ninth grade, but one step inside Fenway and I wanted to play again. The place is greener than imaginable. Green seats, green walls, and grass so green it doesn't look real. We stood in an aisle behind home plate, mouths agape. I convinced myself that given the chance, I could hit a ball off the Monster.

We stood there until some nice people asked us to move on to our seats, even though our seats weren't really seats in the classic use of the word, but rather the standing room only section on the first base roof. We boarded an elevator to the roof, and just before the doors closed, in walked Buster Olney of ESPN. Bryan, who is apparently not intimidated by people on television, said, "Hey, Buster."

Buster, who is apparently not intimidated by people named Bryan, said, "Hey." Then he told us about the Sox lineup changes before walking off toward the press box.

Standing on the roof doesn't sound like a great way to watch a game, but Fenway is small, so you are not thousands of feet from the action. The lineups were announced, and the teams took the baselines just like in a playoff series or all-star game. The appropriate Yankees players were booed unmercifully, and all the

Sox were cheered heartily. The United States Navy band came marching out from center field to play the national anthem, while an American flag the size of Rhode Island was draped over the Green Monster as four fighter jets buzzed the stadium at supersonic speeds. It was perhaps the most American five minutes I've ever lived. Play ball.

The Yankees scored two runs in the first inning when Robinson Cano doubled to deep center, scoring Brett Gardner and Alex Rodriguez. Loud groaning and mumbles of "0–162" could be heard throughout the park.

Then out of the corner of my eye, I caught a gaggle of impossibly attractive women walking past. I stared, because they seemed oddly out of place on the roof of Fenway Park. They would have seemed out of place anywhere but a runway wearing lingerie. The girl in back looked vaguely familiar. "Yo, it's Cameron Diaz!" shouted a man behind us. Sure enough, it was Cameron Diaz, who at that time was dating Alex Rodriguez. With her were the other Yankees wives and girlfriends, who were apparently going to watch the game on the roof with us. But as soon as they appeared, they disappeared into a luxury box around the corner, safely out of view from those of us who would have ogled them for eight more innings.

In the bottom of the first, Dustin Pedroia, a guy about the size of Tricia, blasted a shot over the Green Monster to cut the Yankees' lead in half. Let me go on record—seeing someone hit a home run over that wall is about the coolest thing I've seen in sports.

The Bronx Bombers scored another run in the top of the second, but the Sox answered with six singles and a walk in the bottom, taking a 6–3 lead.

Over the next few innings the Yankees clawed back, and in the top of the fifth A-Rod hit a ball over the Monster that was still going up when it bounced off a fan. If the guy had ducked, that ball had the CITGO sign in its sights.

Tied at six, the game should have had all of our attention. But we heard whispers that Cameron Diaz had moved into the seats just outside the luxury box. There she was, sitting amongst her astronaut wife friends. Bryan and I took turns walking over and staring at her along with the other fans who dedicated the rest of the day to this endeavor. Dad used his ridiculous, paparazzi-style camera to take pictures for Bryan and me, even though I'm not sure he knew who she was. The consensus of the Sox fans who walked by after a sneak peak at Cameron was that she looked awful, and they wouldn't give her the time of day. Sure.

The Sox scored a run in the bottom of the fifth to take a 7–6 lead. After the seventh inning stretch, they scored two more. Going into the bottom of the eighth, the crowd sang "Sweet Caroline,"[5] and Jonathan Papelbon took the mound to close out the game. Papelbon was unhittable, and as the last Yankees batter flew out to center field, Cameron and her friends walked behind us again with their body guard, a man who, if memory serves, stood nine feet tall. As she passed us, Bryan and I both made eye contact, which is to say we stared at her until she noticed. We both felt weird about it the rest of the day.

Leaving Fenway Park, there was a new feeling in the air. Not only had the Sox finally won, they'd beaten the evil empire. Birds were singing, angels were chirping, and I even heard one man on the subway say, "You know what, 158–6 isn't out of the question." There is nothing like beating your rival.

~~~

I mentioned I cheered for the Yankees in the 2001 World Series, played less than two months after 9/11. I'd always disliked the Yankees, and after they defeated my Atlanta Braves in the 1996 World Series, I wanted nothing but bad things to happen to them. Yet here I was, cheering for them to beat the Diamondbacks. I wanted to see New York City celebrate. I wanted them to have a tickertape parade through lower Manhattan. I wanted

---

5. Bomp, bomp, bomp!

New Yorkers to be happy again, because maybe the rest of us could be happy again too.

I asked Bryan about this, and he said, "I was rooting for the Diamondbacks 100 percent. I don't remember thinking, 'hmm, with all this means to the country and New Yorkers, it would be cool if the Yankees won this series.' It wasn't that I hated the Yankees that much, it was more that I just didn't think the game was so important that it had a direct connection to the events of 9/11."

Bryan is probably right. It would have been nice for Yankees fans if their team had won it all, but perhaps connecting the two puts sports on a level it doesn't belong. Sports can be a great distraction, and I'm sure for New Yorkers that 2001 World Series was a great distraction. No doubt it sucked to lose, but probably not for the Mets fans.

However, some readers of Bill Simmons' Page 2 column on ESPN did see a connection. One Sox fan admitted that seeing his "Yankees suck" T-shirt in his closet brought him to tears. Another lifelong Boston supporter suggested that Sox fans should all wear Yankees hats to a game at Fenway as a sign of solidarity. Even the Sports Guy himself admitted to cheering for the Bronx Bombers during their three home games in that 2001 series. Ten years later, he said on his podcast, "That was the only time I ever rooted for the Yankees, those three home games in the 2001 World Series. I just felt like those three games were important. It's just one of those things where you put sports and your biases to the side for the greater good."

Of course Bill could root for the Yankees at home but still root for the Diamondbacks during the four games played in Arizona, which is exactly what he did, even writing in a running diary of game seven, "I'm openly rooting for the D-backs at this point, and just yelled out, 'FINISH THEM!'" Makes you wonder how the Sports Guy would have handled it if the Yankees had held the home field advantage.

They say time heals all wounds. I'm not sure who *they* are, or if they have the medical training to make such assertions, but it appears they may be right. Simmons said in a column that one of his friends emailed him after 9/11, saying, "The Yankees-Sox rivalry is dead, isn't it. It will never be the same—I don't think I could ever join in on another 'Yan-kees Suck! Yan-kees Suck!" chant without feeling like an idiot. Last week put everything in perspective, didn't it?" Simmons agreed, and thinking back to those days after the attack, it's not hard to understand why. But ten years later the rivalry is anything but dead, and chants of "Yankees suck!" continue to echo throughout Boston.

After the attacks, many speculated that sports had changed forever. We stopped calling athletes "heroes" for a while, and Yankees haters were suddenly cheering for the Yankees, but sports changed for only a few months. Loving your enemies doesn't necessarily mean you want them to win, but the way Sox fans reacted to 9/11, it's obvious that they do love those damn Yankees.

Maple Leafs vs. Canadiens

Air Canada Center – Toronto, Canada
April 9, 2011

I hate quotations.
— Ralph Waldo Emerson

I sometimes forget Canada is a whole other country. Sports are mostly to blame. Three of the four major professional sports in America (NBA, MLB, and NHL) have Canadian teams, and the NFL's Buffalo Bills will soon play occasional games in Toronto. When I see the Atlanta Hawks playing the Toronto Raptors, I don't think of it as an international contest; I think of Canada as the fifty-first state. However, as my dad and I continued our journey from Boston to Toronto, that misguided notion began to fade.

Getting to Canada was an adventure. I paid the extra $14.95 per day so we'd have GPS in the rental car, but it didn't really help at first, since the Boston interstate system is made up entirely of underwater tunnels designed specifically to confuse out-of-towners. If I heard that woman's voice say "recalculating" one more time, I would have driven straight into the harbor and drowned her. We eventually made enough wrong turns to be going in the right direction, and we were off down the Massachusetts Turnpike.

On the drive from Boston to Buffalo, I was thankful my father was with me. In part because of the company, but mostly because every few miles we had to pay a toll, and I never carry cash. I still owe him $23.75, but maybe he'll forget. We spent the night in Albany, a city that, thanks to our 1.5-star hotel, I will always associate with the smell of last month's milk. The next morning we were off to Canada.

The border crossing is the first reminder that Canada is not a state. Border crossings are serious business, even the border between the United States and Canada, which must be one of the more open borders in the world. The interstate grinds to a halt at what looks like the drive-thru of your bank, but inside each booth, in place of a teller, sits a very serious, very inquisitive person.

"What business do you have in Canada, eh?"

"We're going to watch a hockey game tonight in Toronto," I said, my forehead starting to sweat because these situations make me nervous.

The short-haired woman in the booth pounced. "The Bruins aren't playing the Leafs tonight, eh."

I stared at her, confused, for the better part of five minutes before it dawned on me that she saw the Massachusetts plates on our rental car.

"Oh, no," I said. "We're not Boston fans. I'm writing a book on the greatest rivalries in sports, and we're going to see the Leafs–Habs[1] game tonight."[1]

"What a boot the Senators and the Leafs?"

"What a boot, I mean, what about them?"

"It's a great rivalry too, eh."

The lady was right. The Senators and Leafs do have a fantastic rivalry, known as the Battle of Ontario. But the Canadiens and Maple Leafs are the oldest rivalry in the NHL—we'd be see-

---

1. The Montreal Canadiens are oftentimes referred to as the Habs. It's short for Les Habitants, which is French for, The Habitants.

ing the two teams play for the 778th time in just a few hours—and the Leafs and Habs are the two most successful teams in league history. The Leafs have won thirteen Stanley Cup titles, the second most all-time, though they haven't won one since 1967, a fact the Canadiens like to remind them of. The Canadiens haven't been too successful of late either—their last title coming in 1993—but even so, they lay claim to twenty-four Stanley Cups, far and away the most of any team in league history.

Once I laid out my reasons for not covering the Senators–Leafs rivalry, Dad and I entered Canada for the first time, and it was obvious Canada was indeed a foreign country. Most of the signs are bilingual, English and French, and the signs in English are worded differently enough to make you realize you aren't in Kansas, or any of the other states, anymore.[2] Even the speed limit signs are in kilometers per hour, which meant I never had any idea what the speed limit actually was.

~~~

Going into this trip my knowledge of Canadian history was less than impressive. My knowledge of Canadian present isn't great either.[3] I do have a friend who knows everything about Canada though, because she is, in fact, Canadian.

Evy Dandurand lives in Montreal and loves the Habs. She also, strangely enough, loves the Auburn Tigers, which is how we met on Twitter. I called Evy before visiting the Great White North and asked her to fill me in on what had happened in Canada for the last, oh, five hundred years or so.

"Well," she began. "New France was colonized by French folks who came to hunt beavers and give Indians small pox."

"Go on," I said.

"Fast forward a couple hundred years, and now the British want in on the deal."

"The beaver and small pox deal?"

---

2. Take, for instance, the seat belt sign. Where in America the sign would say, "Buckle Up, It's the Law," in Canada it read, "Use of Seatbelt Compulsory." Don't you just love it?

3. Quick, name the king of Canada. See, you can't do it either.

"Yes. War ensued, and the French lost, and that is where it all started."

I was confused. "Where all what started?"

"The conflict between French Canada and English Canada."

I was very confused. I was under the impression that there is no conflict in Canada. That everyone plays hockey, shares their belongings, and loves each other unconditionally. I figured it was like Woodstock, without the hallucinogenic drugs. Evy insisted that there was conflict.

"The British were not smart," she said. "They let the French keep their customs and culture, instead of assimilating them as the losers of wars usually have to do."

Evy told me a couple of reasons this co-habitation did not work. "Many of the English were Protestant, while the French were Catholic. Plus the English were the bourgeoisie, while the French were mostly working class.

"So then the English started deporting French people. This is why today you have great food and weird speaking people in Louisiana."

I told Evy I always thought Louisiana had great food and weird speaking people because the French had procreated with alligators. She did not laugh.

Evy continued, "So fast forward again two hundred years and you still have these tensions due to class and language issues. In 1970 the FLQ kidnapped two guys – "

"Wait, what is the FLQ?"

"Front de libération du Québec."

"Okay, let's stick with FLQ."

"The FLQ kidnapped two guys, put bombs in mail boxes, and martial law was declared in Montreal. Then in 1980 a dude called René Lévesque created a separatist party in Quebec, claiming Quebecois were a distinct nation and should separate from the rest of Canada. The separatist party went into power, but their referendum to separate failed. Then in 1995 there was another referendum, but it failed as well."

I couldn't believe that sometime during my senior year of high school Canada nearly split in two, and I don't remember anything about it. Evy told me she had no love for the separatists but felt they were needed to ensure Quebec didn't lose its French heritage, and to ensure equal rights for all Canadians.

"But they did this by passing a bunch of laws, like outlawing English signage, and forcing kids to go to French school. So it's gotten to the point where it's hard for Anglophones to get top-level jobs because they don't speak French. French people can't get jobs because they don't all speak English. There's a lot of misunderstanding, xenophobia, and generalization. And it translates into a lot of aspects of everyday life, including hockey."

I found all of this very interesting, although I was pretty sure Evy made it all up. Canadians are the nicest people in the world, and I just knew going to this hockey game would prove it.

~~~

The drive from Buffalo to Toronto slowly bends around Lake Ontario in Canadian wine country. We passed vineyard after vineyard, one owned by Wayne Gretzky. Near Hamilton a seaplane landed in the great lake, and soon we could see the Toronto skyline shimmering in the distance.

Toronto appears to be a city from the future. The buildings, best I could tell, are made entirely of glass, so the sun bounces back and forth between them and the lake, giving the city a blinding glow. We drove in on the bustling Lake Shore Boulevard. Everywhere we turned people were jogging, walking dogs, rollerblading, or just lying in the grass feeling the sun on their faces. It was like spring had arrived after thirty years of winter, and the next morning thirty years of winter would start again. I imagine beautiful days do not often go wasted in Canada.

Downtown, in the shadows of those glittering skyscrapers, the GPS that had so eloquently brought us from Boston began to struggle once again. We found ourselves lost in the maze of one-way streets that is pretty much every downtown in the world. We finally found our hotel, but thanks to construction and one-way signs we couldn't figure out how to get there, so we parked three blocks away and walked.

We checked in and went up to our room, which was very nice but did not have free Wi-Fi, something I find unacceptable. We forked out the $14.95 for twenty-four hours of service and checked out the Maple Leafs' website for rules regarding camera lenses.

When my sister gave birth to her first child nearly seven years ago, my dad immediately became interested in amateur photography. Now it's his obsession, and he'd brought a lens I nicknamed Hubble. After reading the site Dad realized Hubble was against arena policy, so he opted for his slightly smaller lens, nicknamed Redwood. He loaded up his camera bag, and we were ready.

From our hotel we walked south past the SkyDome,[4] home of the Blue Jays baseball team. SkyDome opened in 1989, and at the time it was a technological terror second only to the Death Star. The dome has a retractable roof, and unlike the Olympic Stadium in Montreal, its retractable roof actually retracts. It is also part hotel, and you can look out your hotel window onto the field. Problem is, occasionally couples do the sorts of things couples do in the privacy of a hotel room, forgetting 49,000 people can see inside their window.

Just past SkyDome on our way to the Air Canada Centre was Canada's National Tower. When it was completed in 1976, the CN Tower became the world's tallest freestanding structure. It resembles a giant toothpick that has just gouged an enormous olive, and at 1,815 feet it makes you a little queasy if you look up at it too long. Dad, with his Kodachrome obsession, mentioned perhaps going up in the tower after the game to take some pictures. Me and my fear of heights said we'd see.

---

4. A communications company purchased the rights to SkyDome in 2005 and changed the name. But since I didn't see any of this money, we'll just call it SkyDome.

Inside the Air Canada Centre, a security guy pulled my dad from the line to discuss the space telescope he was trying to bring inside. As I've mentioned, my father is a little hard of hearing, so when the man said, "Sir, I'll just need to clear this lens with my supervisor, please follow me," my dad probably heard, "Sir, I can tell you are from America, please let me see your camera so I can smash it."

He led us to a desk and explained the situation to a nice girl who told us she was sorry for our inconvenience, that her supervisor was currently on the phone, and in just a moment he would give us the all clear for the camera lens. Again, my dad probably heard, "Ooooh, Americans think they can bring their illegal cameras inside, eh? Once you are beaten by Mounties, you'll have to serve five years' hard labor in the Manitoba salt mines!"

At the thought of having his camera smashed and spending the next five years digging up salt, my father began to beg. "Ma'am, I checked the lens regulations on your website, and this lens is the correct size. The photos aren't for commercial use, I promise. My son and I came all the way from Alabama – "

"Yes, sir, I can tell that," she said, flashing me the hint of a smile.

And just before Dad could slip the woman a hundred-dollar bill, the supervisor came over, glanced inside Dad's camera bag, and said, "Oh, that's fine, enjoy the game, eh." Dad didn't catch any of it and just stood there, ready to beg some more, but I grabbed him by the arm, and we went to find our seats.

The usher glanced at my ticket, back at me, then pointed in the direction of the sun. "Standing room only, behind the top rail," he said.

"Wait, there are standing room only seats here?" I asked.

"Yes, sir."

"And I bought them?"

"Looks like it."

Good grief. I'd ordered the tickets off StubHub and had

passed on some seats behind one of the goals because I'd found these center ice tickets for the same price. Now I knew why they were so cheap. Dad and I were about to watch a sporting event on our feet for the second day in a row.

Standing room only "seats" at the Air Canada Centre aren't nearly as nice as Fenway Park's. You are just stuck up near the lights on a concrete slab behind the last row of seats. And that's where we were, catching our breath, when Dad laughed and said, "Great seats. Think we'll see Cameron Diaz again tonight?"

If you don't count a minor league game in Birmingham fifteen years ago (and I don't), this was my first hockey game, and neither Dad nor I were prepared for the speed at which these guys skate around, particularly during warm-ups, when there are about sixty men on the ice, skating in circles, each firing shots at the heavily padded goalie. It was madness, and I was hooked.

The teams skated back into the locker rooms for a bit, then came out again, flying around in dizzying circles, stopping only for the national anthem. Americans know the Canadian national anthem, "O Canada," because it is played during the NBA and MLB all-star games, just in case a Canadian shows up. It's a nice song, as far as national anthems go, and I tried to sing along, mumbling through the French parts in the middle. Then I assumed it was time for America's national anthem, but the players skated off to their benches and the crowd began to cheer the start of the game. I know this is stereotypically American and my Canadian readers will shake their heads, but it never dawned on me that you guys don't sing our national anthem when we're not around.

The game was not important, at least not as far as the standings or the postseason were concerned. The Maple Leafs were 37–33–11 and, unless someone abducted all the Carolina Hurricanes in the next seventy-two hours, were going to miss the playoffs for the sixth straight year. The Habs were 44–30–8, secured in sixth place in the Eastern Conference. The game was for pride, and for the joy that comes from beating a rival.

~~~

And these two do enjoy beating each other. Thanks to Evy, my resident historian, I began to understand the animosity between French and English Canadians off the ice, and talking to Leafs and Habs fans, I saw just how intense this rivalry can be.

"They are loud and boorish," said Richard Davies, a Canadiens fan from Montreal. "We are too, but we know a lot more about hockey."

Evy told me, "Leafs fans are pretty much the joke of all Canada, since everyone loves to hate the city of Toronto. The Leafs haven't won a Stanley Cup since they built the pyramids, so it's pretty easy to be very patronizing and dismiss them."

"Wait, Leafs fans built the pyramids?"

"Shut up."

I asked Steve Sortini, a Habs fan, if he'd consider marrying a Leafs fan.

"Is Jessica Alba a Leafs fan?"

"No."

"Then no."

Harriet Laclair, another Habs fan from Montreal, summed up the best and worst parts of the rivalry. "I think in general, a certain dose of rivalry is always healthy; sports wouldn't be as interesting if everybody cheered for the same team. In this particular case, the worst thing about the Canadien–Maple Leafs rivalry is the eternal conflict between Ontario and Quebec. Anglophones vs. Francophones. Too often it ends in an argument with a 'racist' tone."

Many of the Leafs fans I talked to shared opinions similar to their French-speaking rivals.

Roy from Toronto told me, "We are loud, passionate, and obnoxious. They are loud, passionate, obnoxious, and speak French."

Jared Wortzman, another Leafs fan from Toronto, said, "A

typical Leafs fan follows his team no matter how bad they are. They will never give up on them. Leafs fans usually think their team and players are a lot better than they actually are."

I noticed this when Dad and I drove into Toronto listening to local sports radio. One of the callers, a Leafs fan, said he had come into this season very optimistic and planned to go into next season extremely optimistic.

Jared went on to tell me about Habs fans. "They have a lot of passion for their team, but when times get tough they stop supporting them. Habs fans are also insane."

As for Habs fans turning on their team, *GQ Magazine* in their "Worst Sports Fans in America" feature said, "Inside the Bell Centre, the only thing people boo more frequently than the US national anthem are their own players. In 2003, team veteran Patrick 'Breeze-by' Brisebois was heckled almost every time he touched the puck; the jeering was so intense it likely induced a stress-related irregular heartbeat."

And as for Jared's claim of insanity, *GQ* goes on to mention multiple riots following Habs victories, including one in 2008 in which fans set fire to five police cars.

Tyler Gallant told me, "Canadiens fans are the life of the party, but the party always ends with an exhibition of bipolar behavior and someone's car on fire."

I began to get the feeling that Leafs fans were scared of Canadiens fans. Not in a their team is going to beat our team way, but in a they are going to set our house on fire sort of way. Even so, the Leafs fans I spoke with were much more open to the idea of mixed marriage. Mike Morris from Sarnia said, "Sure, especially if she were French. French women are gorgeous."

But just because they'd marry the more attractive women from Quebec, don't think Leafs fans like the Canadiens. "I like how much I hate them," said Robert Dicks, a Leafs fan from Welland. "It sounds weird, but without Montreal, being a Leafs fan wouldn't be the same."

~~~

Just over two minutes into the game the Canadiens' Ryan White put the puck in the back of the net, with an assist from Lars Eller and Tom Pyatt. I love this about hockey statistics. The man who passed the puck to the scorer not only gets awarded an assist, but so does every man who touched the puck after it left the factory. Players who retired years ago are still getting credit for assists. The crowd erupted, and that's when I began to notice the place was full of Canadiens. Well, obviously it was full of Canadians, but I'd say 40 percent of the fans in attendance were cheering for Montreal.

At this point I wondered if the Leafs had just mailed it in and weren't even up for a game against a hated rival, but two minutes later the Leafs' Mike Brown grabbed goal scorer Ryan White and began beating him around the face area. Hooks and jabs and hay-makers were thrown, and then Brown got White in a headlock of sorts and slammed the Canadiens' center hard to the ice. Now the Leafs' fans were making noise, and the team seemed fired up as well, but Montreal's Brian Gionta scored two minutes later and the Habs led 2–0.

Toronto desperately needed something good to happen. As if sensing this, Phil Kessel took the puck in his own end, weaved his way up the right side, and blasted a shot from the top of the face-off circle that slipped past Montreal goalie Carey Price. Now the home crowd was showing their guests just how much noise they could make. It was 2–1, Habs, after one period. We had a game.

During the first intermission, a man was brought out onto the rink to try his luck at a shot from full ice. If he made it, he would receive $2,000. He missed but got a second chance from the blue line for $1,500, and this time it was dead center, back of the net. Fans from both sides cheered wildly. When the guy was interviewed and asked what he'd do with the money, he said, without hesitation, he was going to give it to earthquake relief in

Japan. Fans from both teams cheered again, sealing my conviction that Canadians are the nicest people on earth.

The uneventful second half was interrupted when, during a game break, a girl was pulled from the crowd and given a chance to win season tickets if she could identify Leafs' Hall of Fame goalie Johnny Bower in some photos on the JumboTron. She did, and Johnny Bower himself stepped out from behind her to present the tickets. Again, fans from both teams stood and cheered. I struggle to imagine Red Sox fans cheering Bucky Dent in a similar situation. These people are nice.

Later in the second, Brian Gionta added a third goal for the Canadiens, and the air left the Air Canada Centre. No one got up to leave, but the lead now felt insurmountable.

Between the second and third period was a goalie race. Not involving the actual goalies, though that would have been interesting. A bunch of guys dressed up like goalies tripped each other, slammed one another into the boards, and eventually one crossed the finish line, winning pizzas or something for his section of the crowd. Then one of the goalies took off his mask and proposed to Monika, the girl who emceed all the crazy contests and promotions during the game. Again, both Leafs and Habs fans roared with approval.

With about seven minutes left to play, the Leafs were awarded a power play. Trailing 3–1, a goal here and anything could happen. But a faceoff in the Montreal zone went terribly wrong, and in an instant Tomas Plekanec broke away toward the home goal. His stick-side wrister was true—4–1, Canadiens, turn off the lights.

As the seconds ticked down and Leafs fans began to exit, the Canadiens began singing the "Olé" song. You know the one, "Olé, olé olé olé, olé, olé," a popular soccer song of Spanish origins. Why it has been adopted by French Canadiens I cannot say, but it was the last sound we heard as we made our way into the cool Toronto evening.

We did go up CN Tower. I think it helped me that it was dark, and I couldn't totally grasp just how high we were, that is until I walked over the part of the floor that is made of glass and screamed like a little girl.

The next morning we stopped at Niagara Falls, checking it off our list of things to see before we die. It is terrifyingly impressive. We stood on the Canadian side watching chunks of ice bigger than our rental car rush over the side. Then we crossed the border back into the United States and were asked by a serious man with a serious face what had been our business in Canada. I told him I was writing a book on rivalries, and we'd gone to see the Habs and Leafs play. "What about the Blackhawks and Red Wings?" he demanded. I just shrugged. I guess you can't please everyone all the time. Except maybe Canadians. They're too nice to tell you when you let them down.

Harvard
vs.
Yale

Thames River – New London, Connecticut
May 28, 2011

The hater taught hate that's why we gang bang it.
—Chuck D

Call me Ishmael.

No, on second thought, call me Chad, the seasick land-lover who almost lost his clam chowder over the side of Aurora, a three-story catamaran that sped four hundred of us into Boston Harbor in search of whales.

Tricia and I spent that morning in Cambridge walking around Harvard University, taking photographs and perusing bookstores. It was a Sunday, yet large groups lined up for campus tours, hoping to glimpse the window of the room where that guy who invented Facebook drunk-blogged about his girlfriend. We skipped the tour and wandered on our own, basking in a college that's 140 years older than the country it's in.

We were in town to observe the Harvard–Yale rivalry first-hand. I considered watching the Ivy League schools play football. They've been playing since 1875, and their annual matchup is known simply as The Game. Harvard won that first game 4–0, a score that would have set football back a hundred years had it not just been invented. But despite that ugly beginning and the occasional outcry to cancel The Game because football had become too brutal[1], the rivalry continued.

As you would expect with a rivalry this old, The Game has its share of remarkable stories. In 1908, Harvard hired Percy Haughton as coach, and rumor has it he strangled a bulldog in the locker room to fire up his team (who apparently were inspired by animal cruelty) for the game against Yale that season. This rumor cannot be substantiated, but Harvard did win 4–0, setting football back thirty-three years to 1875.

By 1920, over 80,000 fans showed up to watch The Game. Adjusted for inflation, and assuming fans inflate at the same rate as currency, that would be like 862,946 fans showing up for a game today. Yale coach T.A.D. Jones summed up just how important The Game had become when he told his players in 1923, "Gentlemen, you are now going out to play football against Harvard. Never again in your whole life will you do anything so important." Considering many of those players likely went on to lead our nation, that quote is more than a little alarming.

In the early days of college football, Harvard and Yale played for national championships. Harvard has eight, Yale has eighteen[2], but neither school has won one in over ninety years. Today the games are played for pride and for Ivy League championships and to give students an excuse to pull elaborate pranks.

Mascots have been kidnapped and pigs released onto the field, but nothing comes close to the 2004 prank played on Harvard by their fellow scholars from New Haven. Before the game a group of Yale students, dressed as the non-existent Harvard Pep Squad, passed out signs to one entire side of Harvard Stadium. The back of the signs instructed fans to hold their signs up at an arranged time, and when all the signs were held up together, they would spell "Go Harvard" in letters that could be seen from space. But when the Harvard fans held their signs aloft,

1. In 1894 newspapers reported that seven players were carried off the field in "dying condition." This was, perhaps, a slight exaggeration.
2. Princeton has twenty-six. Read that again.

they were in fact telling the universe, "We Suck." Oh, those crazy Ivy League kids[3].

~~~

I didn't know any of this going into my trip, because I didn't know much about Harvard or Yale. I knew a few US presidents had attended the two schools (eight for Harvard, five for Yale), and thanks to watching *The Skulls*, I knew those presidents became president because they were in secret societies, but that's really about it. I never really cared to learn about Harvard and Yale because they seemed so far away, literally and figuratively, to a middle-class kid from Alabama.

If I thought about them at all, it was only with jealousy that those students were born with a silver spoon in their mouths, while I was born with, I suppose, a regular spoon in mine. I didn't know any of these kids, or their circumstances, but that's the fun in stereotyping. If I'm honest, the Harvard–Yale rivalry is as foreign to me as another famous red–blue rivalry, the Bloods and the Crips.

~~~

Saying my experience with gang violence is limited is a gross exaggeration. My one and only run-in came in the fifth grade, circa spring 1989. At the time, like every other adolescent boy in the free world, I was obsessed with Bo Jackson, who played football for the Los Angeles Raiders and baseball for the Kansas City Royals. Looking back, had Kansas City Royals apparel been readily available in the greater Gadsden area, none of this would have happened. But no stores were selling those terrific baby blue uniforms. They were, however, selling all sorts of LA Raiders gear, and my closet was full of it.

It was back on one of those fateful days when Bo Knew that mom and I were shopping at the Gadsden Mall. Well, she

---

3. Not to be outdone, students from MIT occasionally like to prank both schools, particularly during The Game. In 1982, seemingly out of nowhere, a massive black balloon with "MIT" spray painted across it rose out of the turf, halting the game while the officials, and everyone else, tried to figure out what was going on. You need to check this out on YouTube right now.

shopped; I wandered aimlessly by myself, a privilege I'd been granted upon entering middle school. This wandering consisted mostly of walking down to Aladdin's Castle (our video arcade), eating pizza at the Orange Bowl (an Orange Julius knockoff), and staring at pairs of $139 Reebok Pumps in Foot Locker. At some point during my meandering stroll, two guys, roughly four times my size, stood in front of me to stop my progress.

"Do you know what that hat stands for?" one of them asked, his hands in his pockets, undoubtedly holding a knife or gun or throwing star.

He was asking about the Raiders hat sitting atop my eleven-year-old head, and I, thinking perhaps these two hoodlums wanted to quiz me on NFL logos, said, "Of course I do."

"Then you better take it off right now," said the other one. "Or we are going to kick your butt."

At this point I went from helpful logo identifier to petrified preteen. "What? Why? Who are you?"

These guys, as despicable as they were, realized they had just threatened the life of a child who had no idea what in the world they were talking about. "Look, man," said the first guy. "We're not going to hurt you, but that hat is a gang symbol, and you shouldn't be wearing it in this mall."

Then they were gone, and I ran though the mall in a panic, hat in hand, trying to find my mother. When I found her, I was out of breath and had to tell her the story four times before she could understand what I was saying. I wanted her to call mall security, or the police, or Bo Jackson, anyone to take those two bangers off the street. But Mom, like the soldier at the end of *Lord of the Flies*, did not seem to recognize the life-or-death situation I'd just been in. In fact, she seemed more upset at me for refusing to ever wear Raiders gear again, particularly considering Raiders gear made up 80 percent of my wardrobe. Months later Bo would blow out his hip, giving me another reason not to wear my Raiders hat and limiting my gang run-ins to one. But now, trying to write about the Bloods and Crips, and Harvard and Yale, I realized I needed to get to know them all a little better.

~~~

Finding Harvard and Yale folks was easy, even in Alabama. I met Rob Moxley at Vestavia Hills United Methodist Church near Birmingham. I'd spoken to a men's group and mentioned I was working on a rivalry book, and Rob came up afterward and asked if I planned to cover Harvard and Yale. I told him I was, and Rob was thrilled because he is a Harvard graduate. As far as I can remember, Rob is only the second Harvard graduate I've ever met, so I was more than eager to talk to him about the rivalry.

"It's civil intensity," he told me. "Older alums take the game more intensely than the current undergrads. Both fans are remarkably similar, well-educated, well-behaved, but with age wanting to beat the other more and more. The rivalry isn't so much team vs. team, but school vs. school."

I asked Rob if he hated Yale, and he said, "Sure, I use the word hate when referring to a rival, but it is not meant in any terms other than the intense competitive drive to win."

Later I spoke to Kassie, a Yale alumna who is now in graduate school at, of all places, Harvard. She told me she thinks Yale is much more fun than Harvard, and she's glad she did not go to Harvard for undergrad[4]. "I'm always excited to cheer 'Harvard sucks' at The Game, but it's all very light-hearted. I have a lot of friends at Harvard and do not feel strong animosity or hostility toward them or their school."

Keren, a Harvard undergrad, told me, "It's a fun back and forth banter between two groups of students who are usually too stressed out about preserving their GPAs to care about sports and come out to games. So the Harvard–Yale rivalry is the one time that we act like a normal student body and have a little spirit."

Zach, a Yale undergrad, echoed Keren's claims of student ap-

4. How many people say that and mean it?

athy toward sports. "Last year at the Havard–Yale football game, there was a shirt that said 'My hatred for Harvard outweighs my apathy toward football.' Hatred is too strong of a word though— Yalies just stereotype Harvardians as self-focused jerks who don't know how to have a good time, while Yalies are accomplished 'normal' people. Harvardians, on the other hand, think of Yale as a 'safety school.' It's quite common for people to go to one for undergrad and the other for grad school though, so these biases don't run too deep."

I was beginning to think this rivalry was too civil to be interesting until I spoke to Nick, a Yale fan from Boston. "Yale fans are enthusiastic, self-effacing, fun-loving, thoughtful, and loyal. Harvard fans are pompous, entitled, and disaffected." This is what I was looking for, and the funny thing is, Tom, a Harvard grad still living in Cambridge, sent me almost the exact same email, only in reverse.

Chris Casey kept up the hate-parade: "Harvard fans suck in all ways big and small. Picture feral pigs driving fancy cars expecting everyone they meet to relate to how tough it is to decide where to cut back on charitable contributions due to the global financial crisis while they under-tip the valet pulling their late model foreign hybrid SUV around."

I thought maybe I'd found someone who'd actually come to blows over the rivalry, but Chris said no, "never physical. Harvard fans break too easily and are all related to ambulance chasers, so it's not wise to handle them roughly. They also can cause rashes."

I asked Chris about reconsidering his hatred in light of his beliefs and he said, "I think my religious beliefs allow for me to hate those who embrace evil without any moral ambivalence."

Alrighty then. Maybe Harvard and Yale maintain some of that puppy-strangling intensity after all.

~~~

Finding Bloods and Crips to talk to wasn't quite as easy, so first I watched a documentary called *Crips and Bloods: Made in America*. It blew my mind. There is a war going on in Los Angeles. Literally. In the past twenty years, there have been over 15,000 gang-related deaths in Los Angeles County alone. That's five times the body count from The Troubles in Northern Ireland. It's a higher casualty rate than the wars in Iraq and Afghanistan combined.

Made in America takes you through the LA street gang's evolution from an auxiliary to the Boy Scouts in the 1950s, growing more violent in the 1960s following the Watts Riots and the decline of the black power movement, the Bloods and Crips becoming the major players in the 1970s, and eventually devolving into full-scale war as the gangs became heavily involved in the crack cocaine trade in the 1980s.

Leon Bing, a fashion model turned author, wrote a book about the LA gang culture called *Do or Die*. Bing told *Time* magazine, "They're killing each other, and it's getting worse all the time. Their lives are so desolate, they have so little hope, and they are taking it out on people like themselves." Bing interviewed gang members who had never seen the Pacific Ocean, despite the fact that they lived less than ten miles away. As one of the older gang members put it in *Made in America*, "You oppress people until they become their own oppressor."

A few days after watching the documentary, I spoke with Gary Robinson, a former leader of the Raymond Avenue Crips in Los Angeles. Gary is reformed, a community leader held in high regard, and he lives over 2,000 miles away, yet it was still slightly intimidating to talk to him on the phone.

"Basically, I was a gang member," Gary began. "I grew up in south Los Angeles. Originally I was a Raymond Crip from 120th Street, then I decided to branch my community out so I started another clique in the city of Inglewood. I've been in and out of prison since I was thirteen."

I asked Gary how gang members wound up in certain gangs.

For instance if my brothers or cousins are Bloods, then would I automatically become a Blood? Gary said it all has to do with the environment you are born into. "Nine times out of ten, a gang member will have grown up in one of those gang neighborhoods."

"What about the hate?" I asked. "Where does the hatred come from between these gangs? From the outside looking in, they appear to be the same kids, from the exact same circumstance, only wearing different colors."

"It's not really hatred," Gary said. "I think it's more of the reckoning, because they don't know each other. A lot of us didn't know each other, but you became my mortal enemy out of the reckoning. I've never seen you before in my life, but if I see you are from another gang, it's not that I hate you, it's because you're my enemy. So when I see you, I shoot you, because that's what I do."

~~~

Finding Bloods and Crips *was* easier than finding the oldest rivalry in America, which requires some planning, and just a bit of trespassing. The scheduling didn't work to see The Game, but I managed to find an event they've been holding even longer. First contested in 1852 and conducted annually—so long as the world was not at war—since 1859, the Harvard–Yale Regatta, aka The Race, is held on the Thames River in New London, Connecticut. There is no charge for admission, in part because it's hard to charge people for standing on a river bank, but mostly because anyone who goes out of their way to find the regatta deserves to watch it for free.

On race day there are three races—the freshman race, the JV race, and the regatta. The freshman race was scheduled to start at 3:00 p.m. on Saturday. Tricia and I landed in Boston just after noon. We picked up our rental car, navigated the underwater tunnel-maze, and were on our way. From what we'd read online we knew the race was on the Thames River, and we had a pretty good idea where the starting and finishing lines were, but we weren't quite sure where we were supposed to watch it from.

A couple of websites mentioned The Rock, a massive boulder that sits in the riverbank and is painted each year with the colors of the winning team. A YouTube video of a past regatta showed people watching the race from atop The Rock, and using Google Maps we were able to pinpoint it, or at least a blurry red blob, on the banks of the Thames. The problem was The Rock appeared to be in someone's back yard. Surely to watch the oldest rivalry in America we wouldn't have to trespass through private property. Or maybe we would.

Gerty, as we'd named the female voice on our GPS, led us to Upper Bartlett Road, but we saw no signs for the regatta. We didn't see any signs telling us to "keep out" either, so we crept down the road, searching for signs of an historic sporting event. Toward the dead end, cars were lined up on both sides of the road, most of them boasting at least one Ivy League bumper sticker or car tag. This had to be the place.

"We can't just go trouncing through someone's yard," Tricia said, when I told her I believed The Rock to be a few hundred yards behind the house at the end of the road.

I agreed and suggested waiting until more people showed up, so we could at least go trouncing in numbers. Minutes later we were doing just that, Tricia in her Yale blue, me in my Harvard crimson.

Tricia—she of summa cum laude and medical degrees—grew self-conscious as we joined more and more Ivy League elite on our march to the river.

"What are you talking about?" I asked, baffled that she would be the one of us to be concerned about such things. "We have no reason to be intimidated by these people. You're a freaking doctor, and I'm a best-selling author."

"Well, you're a *regional* best-selling author," she replied.

"Thanks."

Soon the road ended, and sure enough, we all walked down someone's driveway and through their back yard to the railroad tracks that ran alongside the Thames. We followed the tracks for a while, like a bunch of overeducated hobos, and then we made a left into the trees where we came upon The Rock and what looked like a massive Ivy League picnic.

Tricia and I found a place to sit on The Rock, which was painted crimson with a massive white H in the middle. The Rock, as with most rocks, was not the most comfortable place to sit, never mind the fact that ants the size of dachshunds were crawling all over it. A man behind us had an old-school boom box, and we all listened to radio coverage of the freshman race, which had just begun.

Harvard pulled out to a lead, but we were unfamiliar with the terms and lengths, so how large of a lead we could not say. The Yale fans did not look happy though, and six or seven minutes later we knew why. The crews rounded the last bend of the river, and the crowd rose to cheer on their schools. To my untrained eye the race looked close, but soon I realized Harvard had a substantial lead. The Harvard crew approached the faithful on The Rock, and as they passed I was overwhelmed by the impressive thump their oars made each time they struck the river. These are very, very strong young men. The Crimson crew zipped past and crossed the finish line, to the delight of the Harvard fans in attendance. In the end Harvard won 9:02 to 9:23, which sounds close, but count off twenty-one seconds and you realize it's a long time to keep rowing hard when you can see your rival celebrating up river.

To their credit, the Yale fans did not despair. They screamed, "Go, Yale!" as their crew passed, encouraging every last stroke. When it was over, we had forty-five minutes to kill before the JV race.

"Go, Yale?" Tricia asked, feeling less intimidated than before. "That's the best they can come up with?"

"Did you expect the cheers to be in Latin?"

"Maybe."

The JV race was longer, which just means there is more race you don't actually get to see. This time we waited over ten minutes before we saw the crews round the bend, and this time, Harvard had an even bigger lead. The Crimson won 13:38 to 14:08, but again, the Yale fans were loudest the final thirty seconds, encouraging the Bulldogs to finish strong.

Finally it was time for the regatta, and hope was renewed among the Yale faithful. The race began, and the radio announcer reported a slip of some sort on the Harvard crew, giving Yale a brief opening. But again, the Crimson crew appeared to be too strong, eventually breaking clear of the Yale crew. This race was even longer than the first two, and we sat for over fifteen minutes before we finally saw the crews. Again, once the boats came into view, it was all over but the shouting. Harvard won the regatta 19:05 to 19:19, a closer race than the last two, but still, fourteen seconds is a lot of time to tick off between two teams crossing the finish line. It was apparent why rowing doesn't pull great television ratings, but nevertheless, we had a wonderful afternoon on the Thames.

~~~

Class hatred is a scary thing. It's easy for me to sit here in my nice home and type on my MacBook that kids in Compton should work hard and buy themselves some boots so they can pull themselves up by the straps, but what do I know about being born into a poverty-stricken war zone? And as for those Harvard and Yale fans, it's just as easy for me to sit here in my modest home and type on my beat-up laptop that they've been afforded every opportunity in the world without earning any of it, when in fact, many of them have worked harder in a day[5] than I have worked my entire scholastic career. What I should be doing is

5. Sure, some kids get into Harvard or Yale because their parents write big checks, but most of them earn it, and judging by the number of "getting into Harvard" books we saw around Cambridge, earning it ain't easy.

making sure kids from every socio-economic class are afforded opportunities, but instead I'd rather sit back and stereotype. Thankfully, others are better than I.

Katy Haber is a Hollywood movie producer who, alongside Ted Hayes, an advocate for the homeless, founded the Compton Cricket Club in 1995. Compton, as in the part of the world where the scariest rappers come from, and cricket, as in the English game that lasts four days and takes breaks for the players to drink tea. I know, it doesn't make any sense to me either, but you know what, it works. The team, known as the Homies and the Popz, made it their mission to curb gang activities amongst the youth of Compton, address homelessness in the inner city through the principles and ethics of cricket, and encourage and promote good and productive citizenship.

I spoke to Theo Hayes, team member and son of founder Ted Hayes, and he told me the CCC is meeting its mission. "We're changing people's mentality in regards to how they view themselves and their value. A lot of these kids don't see themselves living past eighteen, nineteen, twenty; they are reckless and carefree. But through cricket, we've been able to give them some balance and structure. I've seen guys coming in without any regard for themselves or any respect for authority, and after six to eight months of playing cricket they realize there are people out there who are interested in who they are. They develop regard for their own existence, and they start to see a future."

Gary Robinson, the former Crip leader, is doing the same thing with C.U.R.E (Common Unity Reaching Everyone), a nonprofit in Los Angeles.

"Right now I'm basically giving back to my community, a community I had previously destroyed by raising the young men to become gang members, instead of raising them to become scholars. I'll never know what some of these young men could have been—the ones in prison or the ones that are dead. No one will ever know, because no one ever gave them the opportunity. I didn't give them the opportunity."

I hate how I sometimes hate people I don't know. People who are richer than I am, people who are poorer. It's easier for me to stereotype them than it is for me to get to know them, and it's certainly easier to tell them what they should do than it is to help them. I'm glad there are people in the world like Gary Robinson and Katy Haber. I just hope I can learn from them.

Timbers vs. Sounders

Jeld-Wen Field – Portland, Oregon
June 10, 2011

*No one is born hating another person because of the colour of his skin,
or his background, or his religion. People must learn to hate.*
—Nelson Mandela

In the early spring of 2011, I discovered the wonderful world of travel hacking, a method of chasing credit card sign-up bonuses[1] to collect astronomical amounts of frequent flyer miles. By the time I booked my flight to Portland to watch the hometown Timbers take on the rival Seattle Sounders, I had enough American Airline miles for a first-class flight to Jupiter, so there was no way I was going to pay the $900 that Expedia kept telling me was the best deal they could find. But when I searched for reward tickets from ATL to PDX, I came up empty. No worries—I could just fly to Seattle and drive down, but again, no luck. I wondered what the point of having a million frequent flyer miles was if there were never any flights available, but I kept checking and finally found one seat on a flight to Vancouver. I did the math; a rental car and a five-hour drive was still a lot cheaper than $900, plus the drive would surely be gorgeous. I booked it.

I landed in Vancouver in the late afternoon on June 9. I'd reserved a hotel in Seattle for the evening and wanted to get on the road before the sun set so I could enjoy the views. I rushed

---

1. I ask that you not mention this to Dave Ramsey next time you see him.

through the airport to get to my rental car, then hit the customs line. Crap! I had once again forgotten that Canada is not another state. I stood in line, but not for too long, and soon the agent behind the desk was scrutinizing my passport.

"How long do you plan to stay in Canada?" she asked, without looking up.

"About an hour," I said.

Now she looked up, confused, so I elaborated, but like I told you, these situations make me nervous. My explanation probably sounded something like, "I'm renting a car and driving down to bomb, I mean watch a soccer match in Portland with some friends. I tried to use frequent flyer miles to fly to Portland, but I'm not allowed to fly there. I mean, legally I can fly there, I'm not saying I'm not allowed to fly in the United States, it's just there were no reward seats. So I flew in here, but I forgot about the border crossing and all. I mean, it won't be a problem, I'm allowed to cross borders. I'm not saying you have to let me, but that legally I haven't done anything that would keep me from crossing borders. I'm going to a soccer match, did I say that?"

"So you flew to Vancouver so you could drive to Portland?"

Her face waxed over as I went on and on, poorly explaining what was, apparently, unexplainable. Finally she shook her head, handed me my passport, and said, "I still don't understand why you came to Canada, but enjoy your stay."

An hour later, I crossed the border back into the United States, and this time when I told the border agent that I'd flown to Vancouver so I could drive to Portland, I played up the fact that I'd heard the drive was very pretty, and I wanted to experience it.

"Oh, it's a gorgeous drive," he said. "Welcome home, Mr. Gibbs."[2]

He was right. I could probably fill an entire chapter extolling the beauty of the Great Northwest. I've never seen the Rockies,

---

2. USA! USA! USA!

except from a plane window, and my train trip through the Alps was at night, so seeing mountains this big completely dropped my jaw. Plus they were snowcapped, and for an Alabama boy, seeing snow in June is almost too much for words. I mentioned all of this to the girl checking me in to my Seattle hotel and she said, "Really?"

"Yes, the landscape up here is stunning."

She shrugged her shoulders, but the other lady behind the counter said, "I never really noticed it either, until I visited Maryland."

The next morning, I woke early and was on the road to Portland. Within minutes of arriving downtown, a homeless man screamed at me. This would happen more than once. I have no statistics to back this up, and I know all major cities have their share of crazy people roaming the streets, but the ones in Portland seemed to be a little more aggressively crazy than other places I've visited. Maybe they're still angry the Blazers passed on Kevin Durant?

I pulled up to Jeld-Wen Field, home of the Portland Timbers, about three hours before match time and was surprised to see a line of fans wrapping around the entire stadium. This was the Timbers Army, and my friend Justin Zoradi was somewhere in their numbers.

Justin is the director of one of my favorite organizations on earth, These Numbers Have Faces. Right now, they are working in Cape Town, South Africa, educating and empowering college students in hopes of raising a new generation of leaders committed to the growth and development of Africa.[3]

I found Justin and a few of his friends waiting in line near the Timbers Army entrance. One of their cousins, who was now home in bed, had spent the night on SW Morrison Street saving their spot in line.

---

3. I hope you'll check out These Numbers Have Faces' website and consider partnering with them to change the world: *www.thesenumbers.org.*

I asked Justin to tell me some of the best and worst things about the rivalry. He said, "The best and worst things are all mixed together. It's a passionate, blood boiling rivalry between the clubs, and their respective supporters clubs [Timbers Army and Emerald City Supporters]. At last year's Open Cup match a Timbers fan displayed a banner with a big shotgun on it that read 'Keller, Do the Cobain![4] Emerald City Supporters carried flags that read 'Die, Timbers, Die.' There is really no split between the best and worst things about the rivalry, they are all mixed into one."

I asked him to describe a typical fan from each team, in part because I wanted to know, but mostly because this question tends to get great answers.

"A typical Timbers fan," he began, "is male, mid-twenties to mid-thirties, loves soccer, hates Seattle, is probably a little alternative, foul mouthed, under employed, liberal, progressive, perhaps anarchist, lives in a house with six dudes, and rode his bike to the game."

To Justin's last point, I noticed the Timbers actually had set up racks that were labeled "Season Ticket Holder Bike Parking."

"So what about Sounders fans?" I asked.

Chris, another Timbers fan from Portland, said, "They're customers." I'm not really sure what this meant, but in the indie atmosphere of the Northwest, it was probably about the meanest thing he could say.

An eavesdropping Timbers fan behind us expounded, "They are tech nerds who just got into soccer in the last two years. They wear cargo shorts and Teva sandals, shop at REI, and spend summers waterskiing at their parents' lake house."

I was going to ask Justin what REI was, but soon the Army was in full voice, and it was impossible to hear anything.

---

4. I hope you'll check out These Numbers Have Faces' website and consider partnering with them to change the world: *www.thesenumbers.org.*

I am a Timbers Fan,
And I am an Oregonian.
I know what I want and I know how to get it.
I wanna destroy Seattle scum
Cuz I wanna be Rose City.

The Army paused to catch its collective breath, booing and hissing as a group of Sounders fans walked past. One of the Sounders fans showed the crowd he could count to one, and the man next to me pulled a red card from his back pocket and tried to book the finger flipper. Then the singing began again.

Go home, you bums.
Go home, you bums.
Go home, you bums.
Go home!

Of course the Sounders fans I spoke to had a slightly different view of the rivalry. Many looked down on the Timbers - and Portland in general - refusing to acknowledge that their neighbors to the south even deserved the moniker of 'rival'. This is a classic ploy in sports fandom, and when used correctly can elicit smoke from your rival's ears.

If Timbers fans portray Sounders as yacht-sailing yuppies, the Sounders have taken the opposite approach in return. They, "are not the brightest bunch," said Sounders fan Steven Agen in a Wall Street Journal piece by Hannah Karp. "Thanks to their being meth-headed and jobless." I noticed on the Sounders message boards that meth-head was synonymous with Portland, although in the Rose City's defense I didn't meet any meth-heads during my time there. In fact, if they weren't wearing different colored scarves I'm not entirely sure I could tell Timbers and Sounders fans apart, but I suppose that can be said for most rivalries.

~~~

Love Thy Rival

So far I'd seen big rivalry games in professional football, baseball, basketball, and hockey in North America, and nothing had really come close to the atmosphere here in Portland. It felt like a college rivalry game, complete with anxiety and urgency. I realize of course that Timbers–Sounders doesn't have the same ring as Duke–Carolina or Yankees–Red Sox, but after my trip to Scotland, I was dying to watch another soccer rivalry. Besides, *Sports Illustrated* and the *New York Times* had both written features about the game, and I figured I could at least present it as America's newest rivalry. But I learned that's not really the case.

The Timbers and Sounders first met in 1975, when both were members of the North American Soccer League, the same league that brought Pelé to New York in the mid seventies. The NASL folded, but the Sounders and Timbers remained, in one form or another, fanning the flames of rivalry until both teams surfaced again in the MLS (Seattle in 2009, Portland in 2011).

The rivalry has a history, even if today was the first meeting of the MLS Timbers and Sounders in Portland, and this rivalry has hate.

Dave Hoyt, who serves on the Timbers Army board of directors, told Grant Wahl in a *Sports Illustrated* interview, "It's fair to say there's genuine malice toward each other. We have put a lot of time into cultivating the hate over the years."

~~~

I wanted to ask some of the Timbers Army about this hate, but the gates were opened, and they all began to stampede into the stadium. Their seating is general admission, hence the line wrapped around Jeld-Wen. Thankfully, I had an assigned seat in another section, and I had another Portlander to talk to. Jordan Green, my Oregon Ducks friend from my first book, was going to watch the game with me.

Jordan was born and raised in Portland but for the past three years has lived in the arid climate of Phoenix, while his wife,

Mindy, completes her pediatric residency.[5] Jordan was in town this weekend for a wedding, so I bought an extra ticket so he could tag along.

About an hour before kickoff, he came wandering up in an old Army T-shirt, and we grabbed a slice of pizza at Hot Lips Pizza and talked about the rivalry.

"I grew up three hours away from Seattle," Jordan told me, "but my parents never took us there. Until I was twenty-two years old, I'd been to Seattle exactly twice. Once for a Mariners game, and once when we passed through on our way to Vancouver, but we didn't stop, not to see the Space Needle, not to see the first Starbucks, not even for gas. I've been there a few times since, once to visit IKEA and Krispy Kreme, both of which opened up there years before they opened in Portland."

"It's hard to really hate a place if they have Krispy Kreme," I offered. "They should probably open one in Tel Aviv."

Jordan ignored my proposal for Middle East peace and continued explaining the Seattle–Portland rivalry. "Until a decade ago, the rivalry between cities was entirely one-sided. Through the eighties and nineties, the University of Washington was a powerhouse in Pac-10 football, while Oregon and Oregon State were laughingstocks. Business-wise, it wasn't even close. Seattle had Starbucks, Microsoft, and Boeing. We had Nike. Culture-wise, it wasn't a contest either. They had Nirvana, Pearl Jam, Soundgarden, Alice in Chains, Mudhoney, and Jimi Hendrix. We had Everclear."

"'Santa Monica' is a good song."

"Not really."

We finished our pizza and walked to our gate while Jordan finished explaining the rivalry to me. "Around 2000, things started to shift. First, due to its corporate reputation, and partly due to fatigue, Seattle wasn't the place to be anymore. Their

---

5. Jordan and I are both writers and both married to redheaded pediatricians. The only difference between us is my school won the 2010 BCS Championship. Burn!

music scene faded into obscurity, and Portland's rose. Portland developed this reputation as a mecca for food and indie music. Microsoft and Starbucks weren't cool anymore. Even the Huskies faltered as the Ducks and Beavers soared."

I thought about making a joke about soaring ducks, but knew it would somehow devolve into me punching Jordan in an attempt to defend Cam Newton's honor, so I let it slide.

"I think every rivalry begins with a perceived envy. For decades, we were Seattle's little brother, the smaller city to the south with less culture, less people, less money, and less pro sports teams. I wouldn't say the shoe is on the other foot now, but when you factor in the Ducks' and Beavers' dominance over Washington, and the fawning attention the city of Portland receives now, I think things are a little more even. I'm not sure if Seattleites envy Portland, but there's a little more animosity now."

"Do you have an example of this animosity?"

"Sure, take for instance the sign at the last Timbers–Sounders derby that read 'Real Men Pump Their Own Gas.' It was a jab at Oregon, where all gas stations are full service. When I saw it, I thought it was funny, but it took me a moment to realize it was a Seattleite holding up the sign, because trash talking about Portland just doesn't seem like something Seattle does. I think, until this last decade, they would have probably felt above it all."

I was going to tell Jordan that that was the worst example of trash talking I'd ever heard, but we'd just walked through the tunnel into the stadium, and though it was small, it still took my breath away.

Originally known as Multnomah Stadium, Jeld-Wen Field opened in 1926. Everything from cricket matches to Oregon–Oregon State games were held at the stadium, and from 1956–1993 it was home to the Portland Beavers, a Pacific Coast League baseball team. In 2009, the city of Portland approved $31 million in renovations to make the stadium ready for the 2011 Major League Soccer season. Today Jeld-Wen seats 18,627, and it is truly a fantastic place to watch soccer.

Our seats were on the south end, even with the goal, and just below the large section of Seattle Sounders fans that were already loud and would continue to be loud for the rest of the afternoon. But even the Sounders fans were drowned out by the growl of the chainsaw that had just been cranked in our section.

This is not a metaphor. A man had literally just cranked a chainsaw only a few feet from where Jordan and I sat. That man's name is Timber Joey; he is the Timbers' mascot, and he looks like he'd be best friends with the Brawny Man. When not carrying his chainsaw, Timber Joey walks around with an ax, making him one of the top 5 scariest mascots in sports.[6] After Timbers goals, Joey saws a slice from a giant log that sits just below the Timbers Army at the north end, and after the game, the goal scorers are presented with their lumber. Of course it's strange, but if you think about it, really no stranger than paying money to watch grown men play games.

Twenty minutes before kickoff, the stadium was sparse, but by the time we sang the national anthem it was packed and hopping. The Timbers Army sang, well, screamed the Star-Spangled Banner along with the singer, and when it was over, fireworks were launched into the bright midday sky.[7] As the anthem ended, the Timbers Army raised two gigantic banners that read "The King of Clubs." They were cool, though not as impressive as the "Decades of Dominance" banner the Sounders fans had raised earlier in the season. But then the Army raised an even larger banner of an actual king of clubs, decked out in Timbers colors. It was incredible, and even the Sounders fans would have been impressed, had they stopped singing long enough to notice. When the giant king of clubs was lowered, a new banner reading "Quality over Quantity," a dig at the large crowds that attend

6. Arkansas' 400-pound razorback still holds the top spot for me.
7. Fireworks during the day are one of the stranger things I've seen in sports. But as someone who loved to blow things up with fireworks as a child, I can understand not being patient enough to wait for a night game.

games in Seattle, replaced it. The Sounders fans definitely noticed this and booed accordingly.

Apart from singing, not much happened in the first half. I could see the Timbers Army giving their all, and occasionally I could even hear them, but mostly all I heard were the Sounders behind us, singing Perry Como's "Seattle" over, and over, and over.

The bluest skies you've ever seen are in Seattle.
And the hills the greenest green, in Seattle.

At the half, I left Jordan and went up to the press box. I'd requested media credentials, something I like to do from time to time so I can feel like a real journalist, and to my surprise they gave me a pass. My trip to the press box was more about looking for free food than anything else, and the Timbers did not disappoint. Prime rib, shrimp cocktails, and, get this, chocolate-covered bacon! Not the most adventurous eater, I eyed the bacon suspiciously but figured two things so delicious would have to be delicious together, and they were.

The second half started, and the Timbers scored within minutes when a ball deflected off Seattle defender Jeff Park for an own goal. Timber Joey began sawing, though I'm not sure Jeff Park really wanted the memento. Jeld-Wen was rocking, and the Seattle fans seemed momentarily dazed, but ten minutes later the Sounders equalized on Fredy Montero's free kick.

The game settled for a few minutes, and the singing returned.

Burn, destroy, wreck, and kill. Whoa, whoa.
Burn, destroy, wreck, and kill. Whoa, Whoa.
Burn, destroy, wreck, and kill. Seattle Sounders surely will!
Whoa, ooohhh, oohh.

And from the other end...

Build a bonfire, build a bonfire,
Put Seattle on the top.
Put Vancouver in the middle,
And we'll burn the bloody lot.

The singing turned into an explosion of joy when Portland retook the lead as Jorge Perlaza's shot was deflected and snuck past Sounders goalie Kasey Keller. But five minutes later Montero scored again for the visitors, and we were all square at two.

With ten minutes to play, I started to think I might get to see how rival fans react in a draw, but Sounders forward Lamar Neagle was brought down from behind after making a great run into the Timbers' penalty box. Portland defender Eric Brunner was shown a red card for his offense, and when Osvaldo Alonso slammed the penalty kick into the bottom right corner, it was over.

The Timbers Army stayed till the bitter end, serenading their team off the field. I hadn't really seen this before, particularly in professional sports, but Justin Zoradi told me the following day, "We don't go to these games to be entertained, we go to participate. We give our all and expect the players to as well."

Jordan and I began to walk out of the stadium, when I remembered my press pass, and told him to wait for me outside. I was going to go to the locker room.

I enjoy having access to things other people don't. I'm sure we all do; it makes us feel special. However, I am never good at acting like I belong in places like these, and usually I am asked to leave, even if I'm supposed to be there. It took me a while to find the elevator, and riding down to the locker room with some members of the press I was a little embarrassed when the elevator door opened behind me, explaining why they had stood facing me for the entire ride.

I followed the guys who looked like they belonged into the

Timbers' locker room, where they peppered one of the players with questions about the loss. I stood in the back, feeling slightly, make that very out of place. Just as I noticed a table full of snacks, the naked men began to file in. Timbers, straight from the shower, oblivious to the reporters (both male and female) in their midst. When did reporters and players decide this is the place they want to conduct post-game interviews? It was so unnecessarily awkward. Why not add one step to the process, specifically the step of putting on clothes, then conduct the interviews?

I left the locker room and tried to find my way out, but ended up on the field, walking across with the triumphant Sounders players, who were being cheered on by their fans, who were *still* in the stands. Then we walked up the hill to the team bus, until a security guard, noting I didn't look like a professional soccer player, ushered me under a rope and into the street.

I didn't look for Justin after the game. I know what it feels like to lose a rivalry game and doubted he wanted to talk. Instead I went with Jordan to his parents' house to pick up Mindy, and the three of us joined our friend Aaron Donley for dinner at Apizza Scholls, a place Jordan told me has the best pizza in America. I wouldn't argue.

After dinner we went down to VooDoo Donuts, perhaps the strangest donut shop in the world. At one point they sold donuts with a NyQuil glaze, and others with crushed Pepto-Bismol and Tums inside. Shockingly, these were outlawed by the health department; however, they still sell all sorts of bizarre creations, including one designed specifically for the derby match earlier that day—a donut shaped like a Seattle Sounders player that squirts red jelly when stabbed with a pretzel. I opted for the regular glaze covered with Cap'n Crunch cereal. The perfect end to a great day in the Rose City.

~~~

The next day, I visited the offices of These Numbers Have Faces to have lunch with Justin. Eighteen hours later, the agony of defeat was still on his face, and I truly felt for the guy. Nothing hurts like losing to your rival.

We walked through the industrial district to a place called Produce Row Café. Over fish and chips, I asked Justin about violence between Sounders and Timbers fans. He'd never been involved personally, though he'd seen altercations outside the stadium before.

There was quite a police presence outside Jeld-Wen for the game. But the next morning, I read an article praising the fans because not a soul in the sellout crowd was arrested for disorderly conduct. Contrast that to the Celtic–Rangers match I saw, where 229 fans were arrested for fighting. This begged the question, why is one rivalry so much cleaner in the stands? Maybe Northwesterners are nicer people than Scots are.

Joshua Clouser, a friend of Justin's and another Timbers fan, told me, "The tongue is a sharp tool that needs to be wielded well. I choose to take that responsibility both at the matches as well as away from them."

I feel Joshua may be the only one, because both sides were shouting terrible things at each other, just like Celtic–Rangers. There was even alcohol served at the Timbers match, which at sporting events can act as violence fuel, but apparently the first punch was never thrown.

I asked Justin about this, and he said, "There isn't five hundred years of ethnic and cultural identity on the line with Timbers–Sounders. Ours is a modern rivalry, mostly based on geography and the fact that we see Seattle as our 'big brother.' But Portlanders haven't been persecuted or killed in our quest for preserving our cultural identity. In the end, we'd probably identify with Seattle more than any other city in the country."

"I know Seattle hasn't persecuted Portlanders," I said. "But come on, wouldn't you like to shoot just one of them with a crossbow?"

"This may sound funny," Justin said, "but I love the Sounders, because they make the rivalry great in Portland. As much as we talk crap on the Emerald City Supporters, it's all good fun and I would be really opposed to any type of violence resulting from the enmification of Seattle or their fans."

Matt, another Timbers supporter, told me later, "I hate in a fun way. I'd never actually hate someone for supporting a rival team. The rivalry makes it more fun. Without them, it'd just be another game. On game days I make it known who I'm behind, but when it's over and the excitement fades, they're human just like I am. We both went there to have a good time and support our teams, even if they support a lame team."

Seems soccer fans in the Great Northwest understand life wouldn't be nearly as much fun without their rival. As much as it pains me to agree, we do need our rivals. And honestly, we need them to be good, and we need them to beat us from time to time. It makes beating them all the more special.

~~~

That afternoon, I drove back north to Vancouver, and unlike Jordan's parents, I actually stopped in Seattle for gas. Waiting in line at the Canadian border, I dreaded the bizarre conversation I would soon be having.

"How long do you plan to stay in Canada, Mr. Gibbs?"

"Just for the night, I fly out in the morning."

She looked at me, then at my passport, and said, "You drove all the way from Alabama to fly out of Vancouver?"

Why anyone would jump to that conclusion I do not know, but I resisted the urge to smart off, and explained I had flown to Vancouver, driven to Portland, and was now flying back out of Vancouver to Alabama. She demanded to see my hotel reservations, flight reservations, and a long-form birth certificate, but finally let me back into her country, right after adding me to a no-fly list.

Cubs vs. Cardinals

Wrigley Field – Chicago, Illinois
August 20, 2011

Hate was just a failure of imagination.
—Graham Greene

"You're going to regret not buying that."

My friend Mike and I were standing in a store called Strange Cargo on North Clark Street in Chicago, just a block away from Wrigley Field, where the hometown Cubs had just defeated their archrival St. Louis Cardinals, 3–0. I was holding a mesh trucker hat adorned with screen-printed silhouettes of former Bears coach Mike Ditka's mustache and aviator glasses. The hat was $5, and the manager was yelling at the customers that it was closing time. I panicked and put the hat back on the shelf. Walking out, Mike told me again, "You'll regret that."

He was right.

~~~

I've known Mike for the better part of ten years, and though he doesn't like to admit it, we met on the Internet.[1] In 2009, when I was working on my first book, Mike said he'd go with me to Fayetteville to see the Arkansas Razorbacks play, but then he backed out at the last minute, leaving me to face the ten-day

---

1. Specifically an Auburn recruiting site, though while typing this I came up with the idea of *Bro.com*, a site that will help dudes find other dudes to go to sporting events with.

journey to Arkansas alone. Knowing he is a lifelong Cubs fan, I offered Mike the chance to redeem himself in my second book but told him we'd be driving the thirteen hours to Chicago as punishment for his previous sin. He agreed, but this time I backed out and bought us airplane tickets.

On the flight over, I asked Mike how much he hated the Cardinals. He said, "I wish I could say I hated them more. It would probably sound better in your book. But most of my hate is allocated in different places, namely the 1984 San Diego Padres, because their uniforms looked like stomach flu."

I decided not to pursue Mike's gastronomical and bizarrely time-specific hate and asked, "So you really don't hate the Cardinals?"

"Not really," he said. "Maybe if I'd grown up in Chicago, or if they'd had the Internet in 1984 when I first started watching the Cubs. I don't really think about them to be honest, and when I do I still associate them with those weird light blue uniforms from the eighties, and their stupid artificial turf that would burn the outfielders' feet in August."

"They were awful on RBI Baseball too," I offered.

"Wimpiest team on the game," Mike replied. "Oh wow, defense, pitching, and stealing bases. That's exciting."

Mike's story sounds odd, particularly to fans of sports' more hate-filled rivalries, but not when you realize Cubs–Cardinals is what people call a friendly rivalry, or, I suppose, a frivalry.

Will Duncan, a Cubs fan, told me he follows some Cardinals fans on Twitter and they talk from time to time, "but nothing mean, though."

Go back and read that again. Rivalry fans civilly conversing on the Internet. Doesn't the book of Revelation mention that happening in the end times?

Another Cubbie, Jason Leight, told me, "One of my best friends is a Cardinals fan and we like to give each other a hard time, but never anything serious. To be honest, many times the only thing a Cubs fan can do is hang their head and agree."

Again, had this email come from, say, a Yankees fan, it would have said, "One of my best friends is a Red Sox fan, and the last time we spoke I hit him across the back with a crowbar. That was ten years ago, and we haven't spoken since."

At least Cody, a Cubs fan from Peoria, gave me a little taste of animosity when I asked if he'd attend a church where the pastor is an ardent Cardinals fan. "Sure," he said. "Pastors can be idiots too."

I began to think maybe it was just the Cubs fans who were friendly, loveable losers and all that, but the Cards fans I spoke to were just as amiable.

Tabatha, a Redbirds fan from St. Louis, told me the best thing about the rivalry "is the amount of territory that the fans share. Growing up in central Illinois, there were as many Cardinals fans as there were Cubs fans because the proximity to each city and the teams were so close."

Ask an Auburn fan the best thing about the Alabama rivalry, and I can all but guarantee you will not hear, "Oh, the best thing is living amongst all these Alabama fans." But the more Cubs and Cardinals fans I spoke to, the more I began to think they actually do like having each other around.

My friend Brandi, another Cards fans, shared Hannah's sentiment. "Growing up in rural Indiana, there's a fifty-fifty chance that anyone you meet will either be your rival or your instant baseball friend. And then there are those awkward, out of place Cincinnati Reds fans like my Dad."

Tabatha and Brandi were right about the teams' proximity. As Doug Ward wrote for ESPN, "All that stands between these two adversaries is a mere 297 miles of rich, midwestern soil. With each team intent on owning that land, this really is a turf war."

Calling Cubs–Cardinals a war may be overcooking the metaphor, though at least one Cubs fan I spoke to, Elizabeth Kipps, tried to commit an act of provocation. "Several years ago," she said, "I spent some time in St. Louis and decided to wear my Cubs hat everywhere we went, just to see how many people would give me the stink-eye. Nobody did." Try this in New York or Chapel Hill or Glasgow, and I think you'd have a little better luck with the stink-eye.

It's not just me; the players sense the friendliness of this rivalry as well. Jay Johnstone, who played for the Cubs from 1982 to 1984, said, "It's a great rivalry, but there is no animosity. It's not like other rivalries I've been a part of … like the Dodgers–Giants or Yankees–Red Sox, where there is real hatred."

Former Cardinals player Rex Hudler agreed. "Everybody in the stands always has a smile on their face," he said. "I used to get ragged on by the crowd at Wrigley Field, but it was a friendly kind of ragging. I enjoyed interacting with the fans at Wrigley, even when they were giving me a hard time, because they had so much fun with it."

In his ESPN piece on the rivalry, Doug Ward offers this explanation: "Midwestern bragging rights hang in the balance, and maybe that's why the rivalry has an undercurrent of civility to it. People in the Midwest just aren't prone to bragging much."

Of course as far as bragging goes, one team has had a lot more to talk about than the other, at least in the last hundred years or so. The Cardinals have won eleven World Series, the second most of any MLB team, including two in the last decade. The Cubs have won only two, the last one coming in 1908, four years before the Titanic sank. The Cardinals have more league pennants, 18–16; more division championships, 11–5; more MVPs, 20–10; and more Hall of Famers, 11–9. Despite all of this, the Cubs lead the all-time series 1096–1054–17.[2]

~~~

We landed, starving, around noon. After checking into our hotel, we hopped on the "L" train in search of deep-dish nour-

2. Seventeen ties. Weird huh? Last one came in the second game of an April 29, 1981, double-header at Wrigley Field, which at the time did not have lights. The 2–2 game was called after eleven innings.

ishment. On a hunch, we got off at Damen Station, and a block away found a place called Piece Pizzeria. Piece turned out to be perhaps the only pizzeria in the city that doesn't serve Chicago-style deep-dish pizza, but lunch was delicious nonetheless, and the place played really cool music.

From there we went downtown, wandering aimlessly through a canyon of skyscrapers. We stopped for photographs at Cloud Gate, the giant mirrored bean in Millennium Park, then made our way up the lake to Navy Pier, where I inhaled some sort of orangish ice cream treat, giving myself the worst head-freeze of all time. After people watching, we boarded a water taxi and floated up the Chicago River to the Sears Tower. We enquired about a trip to the top, but the hour-long wait persuaded us otherwise, so we boarded another train and went back to the hotel for a good night's sleep.

It was raining when we woke Saturday morning, but the skies were expected to clear, so we hopped on the train again, heading toward Wrigley Field. There is, however, no train that drops you off right next to Wrigley. We had to get off and catch a bus to get the last three miles down Addison Street. While waiting for the bus, we were distracted by a Dunkin' Donuts, its sign a siren song to sugar fiends, so we left the bus stop in a gentle rain, a gentle rain that soon became steady and soon after that became torrential. As Mike and I began to run, the Chicago sky exploded into a lightning bonanza. This donut run was going to be the end of us, I knew it. But just before we met our untimely ends, we crashed through the door into the safety of the donut shop, where we sat for the next ninety minuets, watching West Addison Street flood, and ate our weight in glaze.

Finally the rain let up, and we headed east toward Wrigley, hoping we'd come across another bus stop that could take us the rest of the way. We did, after walking probably halfway there, and we waited with a few other Cubs fans on the soggy sidewalk.

On the bus we passed stately townhomes with Cubs flags on

their porches, and we vowed to look up how much one would cost when we got home.[3] Then we hit the corner of Addison and Clark, and were confronted by that famous red sign: "Wrigley Field, Home of Chicago Cubs."

"Shouldn't there be a 'the' on that sign?" I asked.

"Shut up," Mike said. "This place is perfect."

Mike and I walked around Wrigley Field, up Clark, down Waveland, then back up Sheffield to Addison. He was right, the place was perfect. The statues of Harry Caray and Ron Santo, the rooftop bleachers on Waveland and Sheffield. All of it was just perfect.

Mike ducked into Wrigleyville Sports to pick up souvenirs and was struck with the same type of paralysis I suffered on my first childhood visit to Toys"R"Us. I knew it was going to be a while, so I waited outside while Mike debated the pros and cons of every T-shirt, mini bat, replica helmet, poster, etc. in the store.

Hours later, with souvenirs secured, Mike and I headed inside to find our seats. The bowels of Wrigley Field are not quite as majestic as the outside, but that's to be expected in a park this old, and I think it's a fair trade for the character. Shame on those who've sold their souls for stadiums in the suburbs with luxury concourses.

I absolutely love stepping through a tunnel and into a stadium, particularly a place like Wrigley Field that you feel like you already know so well. I couldn't believe we were there, looking out at the ivy-covered walls and the already drunk fans in bleachers.

Our seats were in Section 142, by the right field foul pole, and we found them still soggy from the morning's flood.

"Hold on one minute, gentlemen, and I'll be right there."

An older man in a Cubs shirt walked toward us with a squeegee. He wiped off our seats, told us to enjoy the game, and wiped off the rest of the seats around us while we took pictures of the

---

3. About $900 thousand for a three bedroom, three bath.

field. I'm not sure if he worked for the Cubs or if he was just that nice.

With first pitch over an hour away, we walked around the field, taking pictures from different angles. I tried to get one from directly behind home plate, but a security guard stopped my progress.

"Can't I just go down and take a quick photograph?"

"Oh, of course, but please come right back."

Maybe this is what they meant by friendly rivalry, because everyone we talked to in or around Wrigley Field was equally nice. Even some of the souvenir shops sold a few Cardinals T-shirts. I mean, the Duke bookstore may sell UNC T-shirts from time to time, but only for burning purposes.

Mike and I made our way down the left field line to take more photographs, and something dawned on me.

"We've got to be close to the Bartman seat," I said.

"You're right," Mike said, and we both pulled out our phones to research.

The Bartman seat is where Steve Bartman sat during game six of the Cubs–Marlins National League Championship Series in 2003. Bartman's seat was in the front row, and in the top of the eighth, with the Cubs leading 3–0, and with one out, Luis Castillo popped up a foul ball. Cubs' outfielder Moisés Alou tracked the ball down from left field and was reaching up into the stands to make the grab when the ball bounced off Bartman's outstretched hand. Alou was livid, pointing and gesturing that Bartman had kept him from making the play.

From there, Castillo drew a walk, Ivan Rodriguez singled, Miguel Cabrera reached on an error,[4] Derrek Lee doubled, Mike Lowell walked, Jeff Conine hit a sacrifice fly, Todd Hollingsworth walked, Mike Mordecai doubled, and Juan Pierre singled, before Luis Castillo, whose popup began the Bartman incident,

---

4. Chicago shortstop Alex Gonzalez booted a potential inning-ending double play ball, yet as far as I know, he never required police protection from enraged fans.

popped up again, this time to second base, ending the inning. The Marlins scored eight runs and went on to win that game, and game seven, and eventually the World Series.

Blame for the Cubs' collapse fell on Bartman, who remained in his seat for a short while, being pelted with beer and soda and verbal abuse. He was escorted out of the stadium by security for his own safety. Video shows him walking through the Wrigley concourse, his jacket over his head, as Cubs fans scream and shove him. By the time the game ended, Bartman's name and address were posted on a Major League Baseball message board, and for a while he received police protection.

Shortly after the incident, Bartman released a statement saying he was sorry, that he'd been watching the ball the whole time and didn't even notice that Alou had a play on the ball. Basically, he did the same thing anyone else would have done, but now he was famous, or infamous. Illinois governor Rod Blagojevich joked he should go into witness protection, while Florida governor Jeb Bush offered Bartman asylum in the Sunshine State. Bartman, for his part, said nothing and has not spoken publically since, despite offers of $25,000 for an autograph and six-figure Super Bowl commercial deals.

I hate watching footage of the Bartman game, in particular the scenes of him being escorted from the stadium. Friendly fans or not, it shows how easy we can turn on each other. You see it in sports, and sadly, you see it in church. I wish I could say had I been at Game 6, sitting near Bartman, I would have acted better, but then I imagine something similar costing Auburn a national championship game. It wouldn't be pretty.

"It's Section 4, Row 8, Seat 113," Mike said.

I looked toward Section 4 and said, "Oh, you mean the seat people are gathered around taking pictures of?"

We walked over and took pictures ourselves, and for a moment I sat in the seat, imagining a foul ball coming my way. The fear, the excitement he must have felt as that white sphere fell from the heavens. Would I have shoved my fellow fans back, making room for Alou to reach into the stands and secure the second out? No, I would have reached for the ball, just like Steve Bartman. Any of us could have been Steve Bartman.

~~~

As Mike and I walked back to our seats, the clouds finally began to part, and Wrigley was basked in the kind of beautiful sunshine that follows a storm. We sat and watched the grounds crew put the finishing touches on the field while the seats around us filled in with Cubs and Cardinals fans. One guy had on a Steve Trout jersey, and Mike pondered giving him all the money in his wallet for it.

Some guy from *Desperate Housewives* threw out the first pitch, then we sang the national anthem, and then we played ball. The first three innings were quiet, which is a good thing, because the Chicago skies were roaring. It was the weekend of the Chicago Air and Water Show, which sounds pretty boring if read literally, but it was actually the things *in* the air and *on* the water show. The United States Air Force Thunderbirds, a demonstration squadron of F-16s, flew throughout the city, sometimes solo, sometimes in formation. Sonic booms filled the air as the jets banked hard, leaving skid marks in the sky, and drawing every eye in the stadium high above the playing field. They'd disappear, and we'd relax and watch the game, only to be jolted from our seats by a screaming jet coming out of nowhere. This must be what it's like to watch baseball in Afghanistan.

Starlin Castro led off the bottom of the fourth with a single. The next batter, Aramis Ramirez, lifted a ball to the left that just kept going and flew over the ivy-covered wall into the bleachers. Carlos Peña tripled and was driven home on a Marlon Byrd double. The Cubs now led 3–0.

The game moved quickly, and soon we were stretching and singing "Take Me Out to the Ball Game," led by the *Desperate Housewives* guy. This, as you probably know, is a Cubs tradition.

Love Thy Rival

For years, beloved radio announcer Harry Caray led the fans in song. After his death in 1998, celebrities from Bill Murray to Ozzy Osbourne have appeared to lead the seventh-inning stretch. Even the visiting fans stand and sing. It's a pretty cool moment.

Matt Garza cruised for Chicago, holding the Redbirds to five hits over seven innings. We even got to see Kerry Wood, once the most dominate right arm in baseball, pitch one batter's worth of relief work. In the top of the ninth, St. Louis slugger, and the best player in a generation, Albert Pujols stepped to the plate for his fourth at bat. Albert was 0–2 with a walk, and though Mike is a Cubs fan and I generally root for the home team when I don't have a rooting interest, we both agreed we would like to see him hit a ball off the Sears Tower.

"Something to tell your kids one day," I said to Mike.

"Exactly," he agreed.

Pujols grounded out to the shortstop instead. I guess we'll be telling our kids about that. One out later, the Cubs had won.

Usually this is when people leave a stadium, but the Cubs fans stayed as a very peculiar sounding song came over the loud speakers. "It's the 'Go, Cubs, Go' song," Mike informed me, and he began to sing along with everyone in the stadium, minus me.

> *Baseball season's underway,*
> *Well you better get ready for a brand new day.*
> *Hey, Chicago, what do you say?*
> *The Cubs are gonna win today.*
> *They're singing…*
> *Go, Cubs, go!*
> *Go, Cubs, go!*
> *Hey, Chicago, what do you say?*
> *The Cubs are gonna win today.*

As the crowd sang, the Cubs Win Flag, a white flag with a large blue W, was raised high above the center field scoreboard, letting the rest of Chicago know that all was right in the world.

Outside the stadium, it was a circus. Mike ran back inside one of the souvenir shops to exchange almost everything he'd bought for other things he'd already regretted not buying. I stood outside, watching Cubs and Cardinals fans pass. Then we fought our way south down Clark, stopping to look inside each bar, marveling at all the fans that were celebrating a late season win that meant next to nothing.

We continued on Clark until we were finally clear of the baseball crowd, still in search of Chicago-style deep-dish pizza. We finally ran across a place called Giordano's, and we went inside. Mike ate two slices of pizza, and I managed one and a couple bites of another. This was the thickest, most insane pizza I'd ever seen in my life—I could have stuck my arm in it and gone down to the elbow. The pizza was delicious, but it's the kind of thing you want only once every twenty years or so.

Back at the hotel Mike and I watched the Little League World Series. It's something we both love watching, I think, for the innocence of it all. We both played baseball as kids, and we couldn't help but laugh when, with two outs in the bottom of the last inning, the kid coming to the plate was already visibly in tears. We were not laughing because we enjoy watching kids cry. Well, I wasn't; I can't speak for Mike. I laughed at the memory of doing the exact same thing.

Your team is trailing 15–2, there are two outs, and you step to the plate, knowing a strikeout means all the blame for the loss will fall squarely on your shoulders. You begin to panic, and the tears well up in your eyes. Hitting a fastball is hard enough under normal circumstances; through watery eyes it's nearly impossible. You swing three times and miss, and then you stand there and weep.

It's silly, of course, because making one out does not cost your team the game. In Little League, it usually has something to do with the seventeen errors your team committed. But I remember being blamed for a loss when I made the final out, and I remember blaming other kids when they did. We turn on our own so easily. Just like the Cubs with Bartman. Just like believers do every day[5]. Just like a church in Kansas.

~~~

A few weeks after *God and Football* hit shelves, the *Washington Post* asked me to contribute a piece on faith and football in America. What I wrote was basically a rehash of some points I made in the book. I talked about how football had become too important to me, too important to most Americans, and I made a few jokes. I was pretty excited the morning the article went up on the *Washington Post* website, but after the comments began to roll in, the excitement faded. I'm not sure if you've noticed this, but when news sites allow anonymous comments, most articles quickly devolve into an Internet royal rumble. It's ridiculous, and reason #1,332 I'm still not convinced the Internet was a great idea.

So I stopped reading the comments and forgot about the article until I received a very interesting Google Alert for my name appearing in a blog post. The title caught my eye: "GodSmack! Fool's Ball." It continued, in all caps.

THANK GOD YOU ADMIT FOOTBALL IS
DOOMED-AMERICA'S "NATIONAL RELIGION!"

Author and Southern Baptist Chad Gibbs in Washington Post notes 16.3 million SB's versus 17.3 million NFL-game-attenders; and admits while in church his mind is on the game, mocking, "God is eternal, but kickoff is at noon." He braggingly demands, let's be honest enough to

---

5. Don't believe me? Pull up a Mark Driscoll or Rob Bell video on YouTube, then spend a few minutes reading the comments. You'll want to take a shower when you are done.

admit doomed-america is a football nation, and football is a religion. GodSmack!

I immediately followed the link to the blog and almost fell out of my chair when I saw who ran it. Westboro Baptist Church.

If you are not familiar with Westboro Baptist Church, I suppose you should count yourself lucky and not read any further so you can remain in blissful ignorance. If you are familiar, you know they are the church out of Topeka, Kansas, whose members show up at funerals, usually the funerals of soldiers killed in war, and hold up signs that say things like, "God loves dead soldiers."

Westboro, it seems, is not particularly fond of homosexuals. In fact, they attribute most of the problems in the world to homosexuals. Homosexuals, they say, are the reason God is killing our soldiers, and that is why they picket funerals. It makes perfect sense, as long as you ignore all logic.

The church has other beliefs as well. They think President Obama is the Antichrist, not a shock really. They are not fond of Jews, or Muslims, or Hindus, or Gingers probably. They refer to Catholic priests as vampires, which is ridiculous because I've seen one outside during the day. Even their website URL is hateful; whereas most churches would use their church name for their site, Westboro went with *www.godhatesf*gs.com*.[6] In 2001, a representative from the KKK distanced the hooded ones from Westboro, calling them hatemongers. That's right, the Klan thinks Westboro is going a little overboard with the hate.

Please don't think I'm comparing Cubs fans to Westboro Baptist members. The Chicago fans I met were almost too nice. I'm saying we all have the capacity to hate. We can all turn on our own, the way Cubs fans did with Bartman, the way many of us did in Little League, and the way Westboro has with everyone on earth who doesn't agree with their ideology. They've isolated

---

6. Figs, I think.

themselves, and they've wallowed in their hatred to the point that they can no longer see the world through loving eyes. They only see black and white, a few friends, and a multitude of enemies.

Jesus summed up the commandments in four words: Love God, Love People. It's something Westboro has forgotten, something we all forget from time to time. I pray it's the first thing I think of next time someone tries to catch a foul ball.

Ohio State vs. Michigan

BUCKEYE VARSITY FIELD - COLUMBUS, OHIO
SEPTEMBER 23, 2011

"For hate's sake, I spit my last breath at thee"
– Herman Melville

"It's 5:42 on Tuesday morning, and Michigan still sucks!"

Five days before The Game—Ohio State vs. Michigan—and Buckeyes fan Jerry Smith is up before the sun, sending out the second of his five game-week emails. I'd met Jerry earlier in the fall, while speaking at his church. After a brief conversation about this book, he promised to add me to his mailing list so I could learn what a true rivalry is all about. SEC fan that I am, it's hard for me to admit another college football rivalry could compare with Auburn–Alabama, but hatred for my rival has rarely had me up before six in the morning, typing out eight-hundred-word treatises. I read to the end, shaking my head, thinking, "Maybe Jerry knows what he's talking about."

~~~

"What happens if they tie?"

"Beats me. Maybe the team that lost the fewest teeth is declared the winner."

My friend Brian Brown and I were cold and wet and slightly confused. Michigan and Ohio State's women's field hockey teams were tied at one goal each, and there were only a few precious seconds left to play. I read a lot about the sport prior to our trip, and thanks to Alex Morando in the Buckeye athletic department I knew a lot about the two teams. But somehow I failed to learn anything about end-game scenarios. Specifically, what happens when the game ends in a tie?

Of course you are probably more confused about why we were at a women's field hockey game in the first place. The answer, of course, is tiddlywinks and gas leaks.

It's easy to name the great rivalries in college sports—Duke and Carolina in hoops, Auburn and Alabama in football, Boston College and Boston University in hockey. But these schools don't compete in just the sports we associate them with; they compete in a variety of sports, both men's and women's. And when rival schools compete in a lesser-known sport, a coach or player or mascot will say they'd want to beat the other school "even if the game was tiddlywinks."

Retired Michigan swimming and diving coach Jim Richardson said it just a couple of years ago. "I don't care if it is tiddlywinks or 47-Man Squamish.[1] Whatever it is, it's Michigan and Ohio State, and everyone is going to pick it up a notch."

If all this talk of tiddlywinks and Squamish is true, it wouldn't matter which sport I saw rival schools play. Football would be as intense as baseball which would be as intense as Candy Land. But I must be honest, I wanted to watch Ohio State and Michigan play football. It's what they are known for, and judging by attendance, what their fans care most about. However, this is where the gas leak comes in.

Go back with me to the beginning of the book—no, not all the legal crap on the first page, but to the first chapter and the 2010 Iron Bowl in Tuscaloosa. That game was played on a Friday, which meant I would be able to see The Game between Ohio State and Michigan the next day if I left Tuscaloosa as soon as the Iron Bowl ended and drove all night, hopefully catching about

---

1. 43-Man Squamish is a fictional sport invented in issue #95 of MAD Magazine. I'm not sure what the extra four players do in Richardson's version of the game.

four hours of sleep near Louisville.

But after the Iron Bowl there was a gas leak somewhere in Tuscaloosa,[2] and most of the traffic was diverted down McFarland Avenue. I may have stayed in the stadium a little longer than anticipated during the celebration, and by the time I reached Birmingham to pick up my friend Mike, the same Mike from the Cubs chapter, we were looking at a straight drive to Columbus, with no time to sleep, and really not even time to stop for bathroom breaks. So at the last minute, I called off the trip.

In 2011, the Iron Bowl was on a Saturday, and I couldn't miss it to go watch two other teams play football.[3] So using the tiddlywinks theory, I began looking for another sport, and I settled on women's field hockey because, well, because I was free that day.

Looking back, had Mike and I made The Game in 2010, we would have witnessed Ohio State trouncing Michigan, 37–7, as the temperature hovered around freezing. That is not a game I regret missing, particularly considering the Buckeyes would have to forfeit it and eleven other victories from the 2010 season because of a scandal that, like all good scandals, involved tattoos. It was the 107th meeting between the old foes, and Ohio State's seventh victory in a row, briefly cutting the Wolverines' all-time series lead to 57–44–6. And while this chapter is technically about field hockey, it would seem a sin to write about Ohio State and Michigan and not at least mention football, so here are three paragraphs and a cloud of dust.

The series began in 1897, the same year my favorite sorority, Kappa Delta, was founded and eighty years before the schools first played each other in field hockey. Michigan won that first football game, 34–0. In fact, the Wolverines went 13–0–2 in the first fifteen meetings, including an 86–0 victory 1902.[4] Ohio

---

2. I cannot find anything about this online, but I'm 99 percent sure that is what I heard on the radio while sitting in traffic.

3. 42–14, Bama. On second thought, I probably could have missed it.

4. I checked, and Michigan's basketball team hasn't even scored eighty-six points in a game against Ohio State since 1997, and that game went to OT.

State's alma mater, "Carmen Ohio," was written on the train ride home from that 86–0 shellacking, and it is surprisingly upbeat. The Buckeyes didn't score a single point until their sixth game against Michigan. In fact, they managed to score only twenty-one total points in the first fifteen games of the rivalry. But in 1919 Ohio State recorded their first victory, a 13–3 win, and went on to win the next three, at long last.

The most famous game in the rivalry, I am told, occurred in 1950, in a blizzard. Apparently suggestions of just calling the game off went unheeded. In wind and heavy snow, Michigan and Ohio State played perhaps the strangest game of football ever. The teams combined for forty-five punts. Please read that last sentence again. Ohio State's Vic Janowicz, who won the Heisman Trophy later that year, punted twenty-one times for 685 yards. Occasionally the teams punted on first down, in hopes their opponent would fumble and give them possession near the goal line.

The Buckeyes scored first, blocking a Michigan punt and recovering near the goal line, where they were able to convert a short field goal and take a 3–0 lead. Later in the first quarter, Michigan blocked an Ohio State punt, and it rolled out of the back of the end zone for a safety. Then, near the end of the second half, Michigan blocked another Ohio State punt and this time fell on the ball in the end zone for the game's only touchdown. Michigan won, 9–3, without gaining a first down and without completing any of the nine passes they attempted. I also do not regret missing that game.

~~~

Brian and I flew into Columbus and rented a car to take in the sights and sounds of the capital city of Ohio. It was cool and cloudy, and rain was expected that afternoon. Neither of us knew if field hockey was the kind of sport that could be played in the rain, but we remained optimistic, then we became hungry.

Brian enjoys those television shows on which people try to

eat a year's worth of food in one sitting, and he told me the show Man vs. Food had featured a restaurant in Columbus called The Thurman Café. It was just east of campus and apparently served burgers the size of Mini Coopers, so we went to investigate.

We parked on a quiet side street in the German Village District of Columbus and walked toward the restaurant when Brian pointed and said, "*Datura stramonium.*" Did I mention Brian is a PhD student at Auburn, studying horticulture? He had a weed identification test the next week and had studied so much he couldn't see a weed without saying its name (common and scientific) aloud.

The Thurman Café is quite popular with the locals, evidenced by the seventy-five-minute wait at 1:00 p.m. on a rainy Friday afternoon. The field hockey game kicked off at 3:00 p.m., so we decided not to risk it and ate next door at the Easy Street Café, which has not been featured on gluttonous television but was delicious nonetheless.

After a quick lunch we had time to kill, and Brian said, "Let's try to find the tattoo parlor."

In December of 2010, Ohio State announced the suspension of five football players for the first five games of the 2011 season. The punishment stemmed from the student athletes' selling items given to them by Ohio State, such as championship rings, and signing autographs for free tattoos at Fine Line Ink Tattoos. Three months later, head coach Jim Tressel was suspended for two games and fined $250,000 for not informing the NCAA he had information regarding the five players that received improper benefits. A month later the NCAA filed a letter of allegations against Ohio State, claiming Tressel lied to investigators and knowingly used ineligible players. On May 30 Jim Tressel resigned, and in July the Buckeyes vacated all victories from the 2010 season. It was not a good six months in Columbus.

Brian and I drove west on Sullivant Avenue until we saw the little house with Fine Line Ink Tattoos on both the front windows. We pulled into the Family Dollar across the street and stared at the tattoo parlor for a minute or two. Brian asked, "What do we do now?"

"Let's take our pictures in front of it."

So we did, and I posted the pictures on Facebook, and people laughed.

I'm not sure why we get so much pleasure out of others' pain. I have no quarrels with Ohio State, and I would have undoubtedly posed for pictures at an Ann Arbor tattoo parlor had the story been reversed. Chuck Klosterman, one of my favorite authors, finds this all very confusing.

Klosterman writes, "Trying to understand why unrelated fans get personal joy from an athlete's brilliance is confusing enough, but at least it feels like a reasonable reaction to have; one could argue that it's akin to why people enjoy looking at beautiful art. But trying to understand why those same consumers might be equally happy about the opposite situation seems unfathomable and cruel; it's akin to looking at a bad painting and feeling happy that the artist failed."

It makes sense with rivals, at least more sense, because in many cases success for your rival means failure for you. If Michigan signs a 5-star recruit, that is not good for Ohio State. If Duke wins the ACC tournament, that is not good for North Carolina. But in a weird way, when we cheer against our rivals, we are hurting ourselves. Let me explain.

Looking back at all the Auburn–Alabama games, the ones that mean the most, the ones we watch over and over again on video and buy paintings of, typically are the games where both teams were good, or where one team upset the other. Blowing out your rival when they are bad is expected, barely beating them when they are bad is terrifying, but beating them when they are good is one of the greatest moments in fandom.

Yet we love to see things like this tattoo scandal happen to our rival. We want them on probation, we want them weak, and I think most of us would prefer our rivalry to fade from the national spotlight if it meant guaranteed wins over a lesser opponent. I think what it really says is we are scared of losing to our rival, because we've placed such importance on these games. We've tied so much of our own worth to the wins and losses of our teams, particularly the games against our rivals, that the games are not fun anymore. These games are serious business, and our team must win no matter what because if they don't, well, nothing really, but it sure feels like it would be the end of all things. I like to think I'm above it, but I'm not.

Paul Finebaum has a popular, caller-driven radio show out of Birmingham. It's performance theatre, and if you have the ability to not take sports too seriously, it's probably an enjoyable display of ridiculousness. But I'm not there yet, and when I listen to some of the callers, I get mad and turn off the radio in a huff. I don't listen as often as I used to, but if a scandal involving the University of Alabama broke tomorrow, I'd have an alarm set so I wouldn't miss the first minute of the show. Never mind that I have friends working in Alabama's athletic department and a scandal could cost them their jobs. Never mind that Alabama going on probation would actually hurt the rivalry and make the games infinitely less interesting than the 2010 game when both were ranked in the Top 10. Winning is all that matters, because only with winning can I feel better about myself.

Looking back I feel a little strange about laughing at Ohio State's failures. As Klosterman points out, it's just cruel, and the more I think about it, it's probably a sinful attitude to have. What would Jesus say about the Buckeyes? Probably something like, "Let he who is without a free tattoo cast the first stone."

~~~

It was getting close to 3:00, so Brian and I drove back to campus and found the Buckeye Varsity Field, which has bright green synthetic turf (no weeds) and enough bleachers to accommodate a couple of thousand fans.

I wasn't quite sure what to expect from the fans at a field hockey game. Living in a college town, I've gone to the occasional soccer match or swim meet, and the passion you see from fans is generally lacking, even in rivalry games. Why we have decided to put the bulk of our fanaticism behind twenty-year-old men smashing into each other instead of twenty-year-old women flipping on balance beams I cannot say. Perhaps it has something to do with the violence of football. Maybe gymnastics just needs to add some form of defense and they'll draw a hundred thousand crazies at each meet?

The Michigan and Ohio State fans I spoke to did a good job explaining the animosity between the schools. Bart Shadle, who works for Campus Crusade for Christ at Ohio State, told me a story from the 2003 version of The Game. "About midway through the second quarter," he said, "we noticed quite a ruckus in the section about twenty feet to our right. It turns out a quasi-inebriated OSU student was openly urinating on a Michigan fan in front of him. Anytime someone pees on a rival fan in public, I'd say it's a bit out of control."

What troubles me most about Bart's story is that the urinater was only "quasi-drunk." Who knows what he would have done had he been full-on drunk.

Aaron Badenhop, who also works for Crusade in Columbus, told me about the Ohio State vs. Michigan football game at his elementary school's fan day. Games that began as two-hand touch morphed into full-contact tackling and eventually devolved into a full-scale royal rumble. "To this day," Aaron said, "I think many of our students still struggle with this. When we teach the story of the Good Samaritan, there is no better parallel for an Ohio State student today than a Michigan fan."

Todd, a Michigan fan from Dansville, told me the typical Ohio State fan is "somewhat red in the neck region." Yankees calling each other rednecks made me laugh. Todd also said, "The first cheer I taught my children was 'Oh, how I hate Ohio State.'"

That's the first cheer, mind you. The kids don't even know who they love yet, but they know who they hate.

I asked my friend John Sharp, a big Wolverines fan, if he'd marry a Buckeye. "You're kidding. Right?"

Marshall, a Buckeyes fan from Texas, told me, "Every year I argue with friends and family to the point of cussing people out."

Finally, Julie from Ann Arbor hinted, jokingly, that the rivalry was even driving evangelism, telling me her church, New Life Church, has actually planted churches in both Columbus and East Lansing (home of Michigan's other rival, Michigan State), and both are led by a Wolverine pastor.

We walked into the stadium just as both teams lined up at midfield for the national anthem; we passed a handful of Michigan supporters and took our seats at the top of the bleachers with the Buckeyes fans. Well, actually we stood, because the metal bleachers were soaked and neither of us had ponchos.

The game began. The first thing I noticed was the incredible pace these women put on the passes they fling around the field. You could hear the ball whistling across the turf—it reminded me of the way cannon balls are portrayed in movies. The players all carried sticks, which look a little like hockey sticks, except the ends are a little bigger and the sticks are a little shorter, causing the girls to hunch over as they run. Field hockey is probably not endorsed by the American Chiropractic Association.

Four minutes into the game, Danica Deckard scored for the Buckeyes, leading Brian and me to assume field hockey is a high scoring game. We were wrong. It was, however, a painful game, as the ball, which from the sound it makes when struck must be made of the hardest substance on earth, ricocheted up and struck a girl in the mouth soon after the first goal. Everyone in the crowd winced and instinctively began counting their teeth with their tongues.

Later in the first half, Michigan was awarded a penalty shot after a Buckeyes defender committed a foul inside the shooting circle. The ball was placed about six yards away from goal, and Michigan midfielder Bryn Bain stepped up to take the shot. Unlike hockey, in which a player skates toward the goal from center ice, here the penalty taker just stands over the ball and whacks it at the goal. Bain hammered the ball past the Buckeyes' goalie into the back of the net, and it was 1–1. There would be no more scoring for a while.

There were however strange rules to learn, like the penalty corner, which is now my favorite play in sports. Penalty corners can be awarded for five different reasons, the most common being an offence by a defender inside the circle that does not prevent the probable scoring of a goal. Least common is when the ball becomes lodged in a player's clothing while in the circle. When a penalty is awarded the offense takes the ball out of bounds near the goal, while half the defenders put on masks and join the goalie in the goal. Once this is set up, an offensive player inbounds the ball by slapping it toward the top of the semicircle, where her teammates are waiting. The four masked defenders charge from the goal with reckless abandon, trying to reach the offensive players before they can get a shot off. There is lots of screaming and jumping and bodies crashing into each other, and it's pretty much the most exciting thing you've never heard of, apart from fire tennis, a game I invented in college that is now illegal in Alabama.

The rain continued off and on throughout the game, and as the second half clock neared zero, Brian and I wondered what would happen if the teams tied. Was there overtime? A penalty shootout? A coin toss? We never found out, because with just under ninety seconds to play, the Buckeyes were rewarded a penalty corner.

Laura Napolitano took the ball out of bounds at the end line, and when the players were set, she whipped the ball toward her teammates at the top of the semicircle. The Michigan defenders came screaming out of the goal like, well, like a bunch of masked girls carrying sticks. Berta Queralt, who my program tells me is from Barcelona, Spain, received the pass and quickly centered the ball for Danica Deckard, who stepped up and hammered the ball past the Michigan goalie for her second goal of the game. Brian and I were on our feet, cheering with the rest of the home fans, most of whom already knew that a tie would have resulted in two overtime periods followed by a penalty shootout. But that's okay. Not knowing kind of added to the drama.

After the game, Brian and I drove around campus (hey look, *Datura stramonium*!), trying to get a feel for the place, but honestly it's so big you'd need a week to see it all. It has to be big—Ohio State's Columbus campus is home to 56,000 students. We did find Ohio Stadium, better known as The Horseshoe, home to Buckeyes football, and on Saturdays in the fall, to 102,329 screaming fans.

For dinner we tried The Thurman Café once more, and this time we didn't mind waiting an hour for a table. Their burgers, I can now attest, are massive. Brian and I probably should have split one. I ate about half of mine and a few fries, and then I wanted to lie on the floor and cry, but people were lined up outside waiting for our table, so we paid the bill and walked slowly to our rental car, doubting we'd ever feel like eating again.

~~~

On the Wednesday before the 2011 version of The Game, I received the Official Michigan Rebuttal from Paul Beaudry, one of Jerry Smith's friends of maize and blue persuasion. It was a fun week of jabs and low blows between friends, the kind of rivalry Woody Hayes, the former Ohio State coach who'd rather push his car across the state line than "buy one #%@$! drop of gas in the state of Michigan," would be proud of.

There were a few more emails during basketball season and one about the big outdoor hockey match witnessed by 25,864 brave fans, but the Olympic sports were devoid of any fan trash talk.

Does the tiddlywinks theory hold up under intense scientific scrutiny? Yes and no. On the field, the field hockey game had all the passion you could ask for. The players meant business, and thanks to our close seats and the intimate setting, their exhausting effort was obvious. In fact, thanks to the small crowd and stadium, I was probably more aware of the intensity on the field at this field hockey game than I've ever been at an Iron Bowl. When college soccer, swimming, or tennis coaches say the sport doesn't make a difference when you're playing a rival, I believe them.

However, there couldn't have been more than a hundred and fifty people at the field hockey game between Ohio State and Michigan, most of them parents or classmates of the players. The handful of Michigan fans in attendance were greeted with smiles, and unless I missed it, no one was urinated on.

In the end this isn't a bad thing. If Ohio State and Michigan fans all cared about every sport their schools competed in with the same passion they have for football, the American economy would likely collapse. The state of Alabama all but shuts down the week of the Iron Bowl; imagine if there was an Iron Bowl every other week.

That being said, if you are a fan of one of the big football or basketball programs, you should make a point to go watch the university's softball team or field hockey team, or attend a track meet. Because sitting there among the athletes' parents and friends, it will dawn on you that they are just college kids playing a game. Heck, you'll probably even see the football players you idolize there to cheer on their friends. College athletics will feel smaller, and hopefully you will realize all of these student athletes train, study hard and deserve our support, but that none of them, either field hockey goalies or football quarterbacks, deserve our worship.

Oklahoma
vs.
Texas

Cotton Bowl – Dallas, Texas
October 8, 2011

Here's much to do with hate.
—William Shakespeare

I absolutely love high school football. I love the sound of marching bands echoing through small towns on crisp fall nights. I love parking behind old gymnasiums and buying quarterback club raffle tickets at the gate. I love flat Coke and stale popcorn and burnt hotdogs men have been grilling since early afternoon. I love watching the teams run out through victory lines and how each year the players look smaller and younger. I love telling the fans across the way that I've got spirit, yes I do, then enquiring about them. I love halftime shows, twelve-minute quarters, and homecoming dances. I love all of these things, and that's why I was a little surprised not to see any of this when we pulled into the parking lot of Abe Martin Stadium to watch the Lufkin Panthers take on The Woodlands High School Highlanders.

My mom and dad joined me for a trip out west to watch Oklahoma and Texas play in the annual Red River Shootout,[1] and at the last minute I decided to include a big-time Texas high

1. In 2005, SBC Communications, which later merged with AT&T, sponsored the Texas–Oklahoma game and changed the name from Red River Shootout to Red River Rivalry, desiring not to convey an attitude of condoning gun violence. But since AT&T raised the rate on my TV/phone/internet bundle, I'm going to stick with shootout.

school football game. It was a bit out of our way, but since movies and television shows are devoted to Texas high school football, I knew it would be worth the drive.

However, sitting there in the empty parking lot, ninety minutes before the scheduled kickoff, I was starting to wonder just how big-time it was.

My mom asked the obvious question. "Are you sure the game wasn't at The Woodlands?"

"Yes," I said. "I'm positive." Even thought I wasn't, and started to check on my phone. While I was looking up the information, Dad left the car to take pictures of the empty parking lot.

"See," I said, holding the phone up to my mother. "The game is at Lufkin."

We joined Dad outside and walked toward the stadium, which looked like it could belong to a small college. And there, on the fence near the concession stand, we noticed the banner.

Lufkin High School Welcomes Fox Sports Southwest for the Thursday Night Game of the Week.

The game had been moved for television, which I guess just shows you how big high school football is in Texas.[2] So after my parents finished laughing at me, we got in the car and drove toward Dallas, searching for Friday night lights.

Driving through the East Texas twilight, we passed one small town after another, most of them dark except for the glow of football stadium lights. At red lights we rolled down our windows and could hear the PA announcers echoing through the town, announcing that a gray Honda Civic had left its lights on or thanking the Lions Club for sponsoring this week's team lunch. Closer to Dallas we spotted some lights and drove through the stadium's parking lot. We were at Kaufman High School, and the game was at halftime. We rolled down our windows and listened

---

2. Lufkin won the game, 30–10.

to the band play, and then a man came over the PA and began introducing the 2011 homecoming court.

"Well, we can't leave now," my mom said. So we stayed a few minutes more and heard the crowd go wild when Megan Thompson was crowned the 2011 homecoming queen. If you are reading this, congratulations, Megan.

An hour later we parked at our Dallas hotel. Oklahoma and Texas fans had hung their T-shirts and jerseys in their hotel windows, a bizarre display of loyalty that I will make sure to copy next time I see Auburn play on the road. In our room, I looked out the window at yet another massive high school stadium, packed with thousands of screaming fans. Texas really is football crazy.

~~~

The next morning we woke early and enjoyed the complimentary breakfast at the hotel. Enjoyed might not be the right word, but we ate it, and we laughed at the Oklahoma and Texas fans sitting across the room from each other in silence. I think they liked the silence—it made breakfast with the enemy less awkward—but my mom insisted on saying "Roll Tide" to everyone she made eye contact with.

I spoke to some OU and UT fans prior to the trip and got the feeling their rivalry was similar to other big rivalries in college football. Most respect the rivalry and hate the handful of fans who take things too far.

Sarah, a Sooner from Tulsa, told me how bad things can get in Dallas' West End the night before the game. "People show ridiculous levels of animosity toward people they don't even know. I have seen fans from both teams taken away with zip tie handcuffs and bloodied faces."

Scott Burkhart, an Oklahoma fan from Oklahoma City, echoed this with just two words when I asked him the best and worst thing about the Oklahoma–Texas rivalry: "The hatred."

Maybe hate is like cholesterol. There is good hate, the kind that gives your rivalry game the added intensity that makes it stand out from other games on the schedule, and there is the bad hate that causes grown men to bloody each other's faces.

Archie, a Longhorn fan from San Antonio, was tight roping the line between good and bad hate when he told me that Sooners fans live in Mobilehoma. Say that to a sober OU fan, and you might get a laugh and a reply with just enough venom to sting. Say it to a drunk OU fan the night before the Red River Shootout, and someone is leaving in handcuffs.

It starts young, as John, a Sooner from Waco, told me. "When I was a little kid, twelve years old, a Texas band member cussed me out while their team was marching into the stadium. I was admittedly giving them the downward horns sign. Needless to say, I ran to catch up to him and tripped him."

I love how it was "needless to say" that he ran and tripped the guy.

Kerry Knight told me how he loves caravanning south toward Dallas with his fellow Sooners fans. He didn't even seem to mind the traffic jams it creates. "I'd say Texas fans are more arrogant than OU fans," Kerry told me, "But then they might be able to say the same things about us. In the end, if a Texas fan needed help or something, I would help them without hesitation."

Kerry was kind enough to ask his Oklahoma message board how much they hated Texas. The replies are best left unprinted, but I laughed at how the thread devolved into Sooners fans chastising each other for capitalizing "Texas."

~~~

After breakfast we followed Scyene Road into Dallas. Traffic was already backed up, and I wasn't sure where we'd park, but thankfully we found a twenty-dollar spot in a grocery store parking lot. I have no idea if the grocery store was in charge of this or if some entrepreneurial man with a money box just figured out an easy way to make a couple grand.

Since 1932, the Red River Shootout has been played at the

Cotton Bowl in Dallas, during the week of the State Fair of Texas. Dallas was chosen because it is halfway between Norman and Austin, though Google Maps told me Norman is actually seven miles closer. We walked across the street into the fairgrounds, and the first thing we noticed was the massive, 212-foot Ferris wheel towering above everything in sight.

"I'm not riding that," I said, to no one in particular.

The fair was waking up as we strolled through the canyon of booths, walking through the long shadow of Big Tex, the 52-foot cowboy with a 75-gallon hat.[3] Workers tried to arrange life-sized teddy bears in a way that convinced people they could in fact make six consecutive free throws on a fourteen-foot basketball goal. My dad bought tickets that could be used for either rides or food, and we chose the latter.

"I'll have a Diet Coke and some fried butter," I said to the lady behind the counter of a booth that sold fried everything. Fried bubble gum. Fried beer. They would probably fry your shoes if you gave them enough tickets.

"Diet Coke?" the lady asked, almost mockingly.

"Don't drink your calories," I replied.

The fried butter was basically a ball of batter—think donut holes—dipped in syrup. I was told to stick the entire thing in my mouth, then bite down. So that's what I did. All the liquid butter rushed out, and I spit and gagged and drank anything I could get my hands on. I'm starting to gag again just thinking about it. Thousands of years from now, when archeologists struggle to explain why our society crumbled, I hope they will uncover this book and learn it was because we began frying butter.

After flushing my system with a few gallons of water, we were off to explore the state fair. Dad still had plenty of tickets, but I was not about to get on anything that could even remotely be considered a "thrill ride," so the three of us got on the sky

---

3. Big Tex has been at every State Fair of Texas since 1949. His 284-inch waist blue jeans require 75 yards of denim to make, though I suppose the fair could save money if they put him in skinny jeans.

buckets, which technically isn't so much a ride as it is a means of transporting people from one side of the fair to the other. Even so, I kept my eyes closed through most of it.

We landed, safely, on the opposite side of the Cotton Bowl stadium and began making our way toward a huge crowd gathered in the distance. Turns out they were watching ESPN's College GameDay, so we sat down on the stadium steps and watched too.

I didn't actually have tickets to the game yet, and I noticed there weren't any scalpers around, becoming a little worried that this trip to Texas would end in missing both of the things we'd come to see. Finally a guy walked by with one ticket in his hand. I chased him down, asked how much, and then asked him to wait just a minute. He was asking more than I wanted to pay, and I wouldn't be able to buy tickets for my parents, so I asked them what they thought. They said to buy it; they'd just have a date at the fair. So I paid the man.

I believe football that starts before noon is an abomination, and kickoff for the 2011 Red River Gun Violence Bowl was set for 11:00AM. I told my parents to have fun on their date and went to find my seat, which was high in the upper deck (or low in the stratosphere), among the Oklahoma faithful.

The Cotton Bowl divides tickets for the game fifty-fifty, and you can easily see on the fifty-yard line where the burnt orange stops and the crimson begins. This made my baby blue Manchester City T-shirt stand out a little more than I wanted, but it also provided an incredible atmosphere for a rivalry game.

Across the field I could see Bevo, UT's Texas longhorn steer mascot. There is a great legend about how Bevo got his name, involving Texas A&M students kidnapping the steer in 1916 and branding him with the 13–0 score from the 1915 game. Texas students turned the 1 and the 3 into a B, the – into an E, inserted a V, and voila, BEVO. Sadly this story may not hold up to intense historical scrutiny.

Even without embellishment, Bevo's history is pretty great. The first Bevo was fattened up and fed to the team at a 1920 football banquet. Bevo II charged an SMU cheerleader. Bevo III escaped and terrorized the UT campus for two days.[4] Bevo IV charged a parked car. And Bevo V charged and scattered the Baylor band. Unfortunately, Bevo XIV just sat in the end zone, giving me nothing interesting to write about here.

In the end zone below me I could see the official mascot of OU, the Sooner Schooner, a small Conestoga wagon pulled by two white ponies. The Schooner is driven by the RUF/NEKS, Oklahoma's all-male spirit organization. The RUF/NEK queen rides shotgun, and when the Sooners score in home games, the Schooner is driven onto the field in a giant circle, crossing the midfield stripe and returning to the end zone.

I asked the Sooners fan next to me if the Schooner would be riding after scores in the Cotton Bowl, and he said, "No, just home games. The '85 Orange Bowl kind of changed things."

"What happened there?" I asked.

"We were playing Washington, and it was 14–14 in the second half. We had a short field goal, twenty yards or so, and made it. The Schooner took off around the field to celebrate, not knowing there was an illegal procedure call against the Sooners. And because the field was so wet from all the rain, the Schooner got stuck. They gave us another fifteen-yard penalty for unsportsmanlike conduct, and then we missed the much longer field goal. Washington went on to win the game, and the Schooner now only rides at home."[5]

The pregame festivities began as the Pride of Oklahoma Marching Band took the field, marching around in formation, whipping their fans into a frenzy. Next the Texas band was led

---

4. Two days! I love that students went to bed that first night knowing there was a raging cow loose on their campus.

5. I'd be remiss to not mention the Sooner Schooner Mooner in 1993, when the wagon tipped over, dumping the RUF/NEK queen upside down on the turf, her dress flying over her head, her underwear back in the dorm room.

onto the field by their drum major, who did a line dance at midfield, whipping their fans into an equal and identical frenzy.

Then the public address announcer spoke up and said something to the effect of, "Ladies and gentlemen, please rise, respectfully remove your hats, place your hands over your hearts, and join in singing …" We all stood, prepared to sing the national anthem, but the PA announcer continued, "… as the Longhorn marching band plays 'The Eyes of Texas!'" The OU fans sat down as fast as humanly possible, and to show their displeasure at being punk'd, booed so loudly that I didn't hear the first note of the song. It was awesome.

Of course Oklahoma was able to pay Texas back every time the UT crowd began their "Texas, Horns" cheer. One side of the UT section would yell "Texas!" and at the same time as the other side responded "Horns!" the entire OU section would yell "Sucks!" To an impartial observer like me, it sounded like the entire stadium had organized one giant "Texas Sucks!" cheer.

~~~

This was the 106th meeting between Texas and Oklahoma; the first was in 1900. Texas won that inaugural contest 28–2, in a game the Austin American-Statesmen referred to as a "practice game."

The Statesmen reported of that first game, "While Oklahoma should be given credit for the stiffness of her center trio, the fact that the Varsity backs made but small headway at these points is partly due to the Varsity backs themselves. They had not the life and dash that is necessary to successful line plunging, and they failed to heed Coach Thompson's oft repeated admonition to hit the line low and with speed, and the consequence was that when they got to the line they did not have the necessary momentum to plunge on through."

This sounds a bit more like a plumber's manual than a football report.

Texas dominated early, winning twenty-nine of the first forty-two matchups. Then in 1947 Bud Wilkinson became the head coach at Oklahoma. Under Wilkinson Oklahoma won thirteen straight Big 8 titles and three national championships, and beat Texas nine out of ten games from 1948–1957.[6]

It was a former Oklahoma quarterback under Wilkinson, Darrell Royal, who swung things back toward the orange side of the rivalry. Taking the helm of the Longhorns coaching staff in 1957, Royal went 12–2 against the Sooners in his first fourteen attempts, giving the Longhorns three national titles. Texas' stadium was later named Darrell K. Royal–Texas Memorial Stadium, after the one-time Sooners QB.

The rivalry really began to heat up during the 1970s, when Barry Switzer took the helm at Oklahoma. Before the 1976 game, Royal accused Switzer of sending spies to closed practices at Texas Stadium. On game day, President Gerald Ford escorted both coaches to midfield for the coin toss. Swizter and Royal spoke to Ford, but not to each other.

In the eighties[7] guys like Brian Bosworth kept things interesting. Bosworth once said, "I don't like Texas. I don't like the city of Austin. And I don't like the color orange. It reminds me of puke."

And now the game is over a hundred years old, with Texas leading the all-time series 59–41–5. The rivalry has already seen it share of great games and blowouts in the first decade of the new millennium, usually between two highly ranked opponents. This year was no different. Texas entered the game ranked #11; Oklahoma was #3. Play ball.

~~~

The game began, and in the first quarter Oklahoma kicked two field goals, Texas one. A sleepy first fifteen minutes, but in the game's defense, it was still morning. (I believe football that starts before noon is an abomination, and kickoff for the 2011

6. From 1953–1957 OU won forty-seven straight games, a record that still stands to this day.
7. The 1984 matchup is considered by some the greatest game in the rivalry; #1 Texas tied #3 Oklahoma, 15–15.

Red River Gun Violence Bowl was set for 11:00 a.m.)

As the second quarter began, Oklahoma quarterback Landry Jones hit Kenny Stills on a nineteen-yard touchdown pass to give the Sooners a 13–3 lead. Three minutes later, Jones hit Ryan Broyles on a five-yard touchdown pass, and it was 20–3, Sooners. The next eight or nine minutes passed without incident, but with just a few minutes to play before halftime, Texas quarterback David Ash was hurried and threw a pass up for grabs. Unfortunately for Ash it was grabbed by OU defender Demontre Hurst, who took the interception back fifty-five yards for the score. 27–3, Sooners.

The game was over, and it wasn't even halftime. A few UT fans left early for halftime concessions, some probably just kept walking. But then Texas running back Foswhitt "Fozzy" Whittaker took the ensuing kickoff, darted straight up the middle, and once he juked the kicker at the twenty-five-yard line, there was nothing but green grass in front of him. A 100-yard return, and it was 27–10, Sooners, the orange side of the stadium now buzzing. If they could hold the Sooners for the final two minutes, Texas would get the ball back to start the second half and just might make a game of it.

But OU's Landry Jones's passing was surgical, and with less than forty seconds to play he connected to Still again for a fourteen-yard touchdown. It was 34–10 at the half, and the only question now was how many more points OU would score.

Texas took the ball to start the half, fumbled, and Oklahoma defender David King scooped up the ball and ran nineteen yards to make the score 41–10. The Sooners would score twice more before taking their foot off the gas at 55. Texas scored late, making the final score of the 106th Gun Violence Bowl 55–17.

By the time Texas scored their last touchdown, I had ventured out of the stadium to see if there was anything more interesting going on. There was. I saw an Oklahoma and Texas fan nearly come to blows. But what was weird was neither of them was watching the game. I know it was all but over, but there were tons of people in OU and UT shirts who spent most of the game at the fair, eating fried cotton candy and trying to win a stuffed animal so big they'd have to rent a truck to take it home. I thought it was a little bizarre.

I called my mom and dad and told them to meet me at the car, and a few minutes later they came walking up, both eating candied apples, Mom with a stuffed animal Dad had won for her. They looked like high school kids on a date, and even though I didn't get them tickets to the game, I think they had a great time. It's hard to beat a fair.

~~~

Driving home the next day, I called Tricia, and she asked how the game was.

"It was okay," I said.

"Just okay?" she asked, sounding a little perturbed that I'd spent a lot of money to watch a game that was just okay.

"I mean, it was great and all. The atmosphere, the fans, the fair, it was all really cool and I'm glad I saw it, but I just didn't care about it."

It's something I noticed as I went from rivalry to rivalry. I just didn't care about it the way the fans of the teams did. Not even close. I understand that Texas fans probably still get nauseated when they think about the 55–17 score. And I know Oklahoma fans are probably still watching their DVR recording of that same game. But it was just another Oklahoma–Texas game to me. They play one every year. They'll play it again next year.

I can tell you the winner of the Iron Bowl at least back to the 1950s and can list most of the scores. So can most of my friends. But when I ask them to tell me the winners of the last ten Ohio State–Michigan games or the last ten Red River Shootouts, they struggle. Go back farther than that and they wouldn't have a clue.

I've always convinced myself that the rest of the nation cares about the Auburn–Alabama game the way I do. I think when

Auburn wins, everyone takes notice, and everyone thinks great things about Auburn, which means they are thinking great things about me, because I'm connected to Auburn. Conversely, when Auburn loses, the nation is laughing at us, which means they are also laughing at me. Truth is, for most people the Auburn–Alabama game is just another score that flashes on the bottom of the screen in late November. They may take note of who won, particularly if they are degenerate gamblers, but that's really it.

Realizing that the rest of the world doesn't care about your rivalry is a great thing. It puts it in perspective, and I think knowing the game isn't quite as big as you thought helps you enjoy it that much more. This became even clearer six days later on a cool October night in the metropolis of Hokes Bluff, Alabama.

Glencoe
vs.
Hokes Bluff

Hokes Bluff Eagles Stadium – Hokes Bluff, Alabama
October 14, 2011

Hate your next-door neighbor, but don't forget to say grace.
—Barry McGuire

"I want you to close your eyes for a minute."

I'm standing in the corner of the visitor's locker room at Hokes Bluff Eagles Stadium, trying my best to stay out of the way, as Glencoe head coach Lee Ozmint addresses his team. I'm not sure if his speech is meant only for them or for everyone in the room. To be safe, I close my eyes too.

"I want you to think back to when you were little. When you were out in your back yard, dreaming about throwing a game-winning pass or making a game-saving tackle."

My mind drifts back, and there I am, a little chubby, a lot uncoordinated, throwing passes to imaginary receivers, celebrating each touchdown with an embarrassing dance.

"Now think about who you were playing against in those dreams. It wasn't Weaver, and it wasn't Piedmont. It was Hokes Bluff."

I'm bouncing on my toes a little. I can feel goose bumps forming on my neck, and my stomach churns like I had butterflies for dinner.

"It was Hokes Bluff because this is the game people remember. This is the game people talk about twenty, thirty years from now. This is the one chance you get to beat your archrival, and seniors, this is your last chance."

Now my eyes are open, scanning the room for an extra pair of shoulder pads and a helmet no one is using. I just want to go in for the opening kickoff. I want to run down the field and hit someone in green as hard as I can. I don't care if my opponent is sixteen and I'm thirty-three. I don't care that my hair is graying and I haven't run full-speed in at least ten years. Just one play, that's all I want.

Coach Ozmint ups the ante. "My father, Ed Ozmint, is here from South Carolina tonight. He is eighty-one years old, and I'm not sure how many more times he will get to watch me coach. That's why when this game is over, I want to be able to hand him the game ball."

I'm foaming at the mouth. I don't need pads or a helmet. I don't even need a door. I'm ready to run through the concrete walls of the locker room. I'm ready to leave it all on the field.

Coach is yelling now, and the players are on their feet, bouncing up and down. There is screaming and jumping and the crack of helmets butting together. The door swings open, and the Glencoe Yellow Jackets are ready to fly out like someone poked their nest with a stick. Hokes Bluff doesn't know what's coming.

~~~

I'd come to town on Thursday afternoon, one day before Glencoe and Hokes Bluff were set to play for the sixty-eighth time. It was three o'clock, and school was just letting out as I pulled into the parking lot of Glencoe High School, my alma mater. The team was already practicing, loud speakers blaring music to prepare them for the noise they'd face in Hokes Bluff the next day. I stood by the fence, and my cousin Tommy Stanley, who coaches tight ends, walked over and said hello.

Purple storm clouds rolled in, and I felt the first drops of rain on my arm as practice wrapped up. The team jogged to the locker room, and I followed closely behind. Inside, Tommy introduced me to the rest of the coaching staff. I said hello, then sat in the corner and listened to them talk about tomorrow's game. It was a big one, even without the rivalry. Glencoe was 5–2; Hokes Bluff was 4–3. A win could propel either team into the state playoffs, while a loss would be hard to overcome.

Glencoe principal Charlton Giles walked into the office and informed Coach Ozmint that one of his players would not be available for the Hokes Bluff game because he'd started a fight in the lunchroom.[1] This turned the conversation from football to the worst fights the coaches had ever broken up at school. It made me miss the excitement of running to watch a fight at school and made me thankful I don't have job where I could accidentally get punched in the face. The coaches were still telling stories when I left the locker room thirty minutes later.

~~~

I left the fieldhouse and stopped by the Big Chief Restaurant, a multicolored A-frame building with two giant arrows holding up its sign out front. I ordered the same thing I've ordered since I was a kid, a grape milkshake, and then I was off to spend a few hours at the Gadsden Public Library. Not the most exciting way to spend a Thursday evening, but there were things I wanted to know, and my parents refused to volunteer any information.

After about thirty minutes of scanning microfilm, I finally found it in the September 13, 1973, edition of the *Gadsden Times*.

> HOKES BLUFF – State Fire Marshall W.B. Houston has been called in to investigate a fire which destroyed an estimated 25 percent of the Hokes Bluff High School fieldhouse last night.
>
> Considerable water damage resulted when the Hokes

---

1. I don't think Nick Saban or Gene Chizik ever have to deal with stuff like this.

Bluff Volunteer Fire Department extinguished the fire before it did further damage according to Ray Campbell, principal. The damage to the frame upper section of the cement block building resulted when wood, collected for a bonfire, apparently was ignited near the structure.

The wood was collected as competition between classes for a rally before the football game between Hokes Bluff and Glencoe scheduled for tomorrow night.

Here in black and white, facts to a story I'd heard all my life though never truly believed. Then, this appeared in the following day's paper:

HOKES BLUFF – Fire Probe Continues – No arrests have been made in connection with the apparent arson which resulted in a portion of the Hokes Bluff High School fieldhouse locker room being burned Wednesday night. There are some suspects in the case, according to school officials.

A car which was thought to be owned by the suspects was found near the scene, apparently the victim of mechanical failure. When the car was claimed by the owner, a student at Glencoe High, some green and white paint was on it, officials said.

I printed the two columns, read them again, and laughed a little louder than you are supposed to in a library. That student is my father, Alan Gibbs. That car which was the victim of mechanical failure and was later painted green was his blue 1970 Dodge Charger. And that fire, which burned down parts of the Hokes Bluff fieldhouse, was the result of my dad and some friends thinking it would be funny to light Hokes Bluffs' pep rally bonfire twenty-four hours early.

"Glencoe wasn't going to have a bonfire for the Hokes Bluff game," my dad finally told me, "and we figured Hokes Bluff shouldn't have one either. So we snuck over there and lit it one night early."

There were allegations that perhaps some Glencoe football players had been involved in the alleged arson, but no one was suspended for the game, and Glencoe won 14–0, going on to an undefeated season and the 2-A state title. As for the fire, my dad told me State Fire Marshall W. B. Houston didn't seem too interested in prosecuting a bunch of kids for a high school prank, concluding that since the bonfire was built so close to the field-house, my dad and his friends actually saved Hokes Bluff the embarrassment of burning it down themselves.

~~~

On game day I ventured into enemy territory, stepping foot inside Hokes Bluff High School for the first time in my life. I'd always imagined the inside of HBHS looked a little like the inside of the Death Star. Dark, sterile hallways, and possibly Storm Troopers, but it looked like any other high school—the front doors opened into a lobby full of trophy cases and a sign requesting all visitors check in at the office. Principle Scott Calhoun had cleared me to attend the pep rally, and I walked into his office with fear and trembling. It was the first time I'd been in a principal's office in fifteen years.

Some of my first memories are of Glencoe High School pep rallies. My aunt Tammy was a member of the Glencoe marching band, and Fridays my mom and grandma Helen would take me to watch the old gymnasium explode with school spirit. For Hokes Bluff week, green spray-painted chickens would always find their way onto the gym floor, and I can't tell you how many times I've heard about legendary Glencoe coach Lyle Darnell wringing a chicken's neck during a pep rally to fire up his team.

I visited with Coach Darnell, who never lost to Hokes Bluff

in his twelve seasons at Glencoe, while writing this chapter. When I brought up this story he laughed and assured me the chicken was only knocked unconscious, and that it came to sometime after the pep rally. Coach showed me some old newspaper clippings and recounted his favorite memories from the rivalry. By the time I left I could tell the stroll down memory lane had fired him up a bit. It had been thirty-three years since he'd coached a game at Glencoe, but as I was leaving he said, "I wish we were playing them tonight."

My mom always told me about "ghost walks" at Glencoe the day of the Hokes Bluff game. After the morning bell rang, no one, not teacher nor student, would utter a word. Lessons were given on the blackboard, and lunch was eaten in total silence. Not until the first drum beat of the pep rally would the student body unleash a racket that could raise the dead. One of my favorite high school memories is of busting out of homeroom, running through the halls, banging on lockers and chanting, "Ruff the Bluff!" It's a shame there are not more pep rallies in the real world.

Principal Calhoun escorted me to the lunchroom, where the pep rally was held. The lights were off, a smoke machine fogged up the room, and the eerie glow of red lights gave the room the creepy vibe I'd always imagined Hokes Bluff High School would have. Speaking of creepy vibes, I stood in the back of the room trying to go unnoticed but probably looking like a windowless van owner who had snuck into the high school.

Soon the students came in, and I hated them all. I mean, the ones who stood in the back and talked to me were nice enough, but still, these were Hokes Bluff kids, and I had to hate them. I'd been raised to hate them.

~~~

My grandpa James, perhaps the nicest man I ever knew, couldn't stand Hokes Bluff. Just a few years before he passed away he went to watch my cousin Lexie play basketball for Glencoe in the county tournament. As he was weakened from a recent heart attack, everyone thought it best Grandpa didn't attempt to climb the bleachers, so a seat was arranged for him on the floor. When Grandpa James realized this meant he'd be sitting next to a man in Hokes Bluff green, he turned to my uncle Wayne and said, "I think I'm healthy enough to climb."

I learned at an early age that no one from Hokes Bluff was to be trusted. They were all left handed[2], and they all had one of five last names (Young, Reeves, Shields, Marbut, or Noah), and if that's not reason enough to hate someone, I don't know what is.

In high school, most weekends brought fights between Glencoe and Hokes Bluff kids, or at least rumors of fights. None involving me, mind you. I was never much of a fighter, but it seemed everyone in Hokes Bluff wanted to kill my friend Ryan Cothran at one time or another. I remember cruising Broad Street in Gadsden on Saturday nights, trying to meet girls, but trying harder to avoid a car full of Hokes Bluff guys who wanted Ryan to meet their fists.

When we graduated, we all ended up at the local junior college, and we got to know each other, and then we were all friends. It was strange, because I'd been told they eat kittens and refuse to help old ladies across the street, but apparently they were just like us. I even dated a Hokes Bluff girl for a while, but we broke up around the time Hokes Bluff won the 2001 state championship. I'm not saying the two things were related, but I'm not saying they weren't.

The problem today is the students are learning way too early that their rivals don't eat kittens, or any pets for that matter. They friend each other on Facebook, follow each other on Twitter, play with each other on traveling baseball and softball teams, and by the time they are supposed to hate each other, they sort of like each other.

---

2. I have no census data to back this up, but my friend JT Hornbuckle (Glencoe class of 1999), swears it's true.

Hokes Bluff head coach Mike Robertson told the Gadsden Times in the days leading up to this year's game that "a lot of people compare it to Alabama and Auburn," but added, "I don't think it's as big as it used to be."

Robertson said it's partly because these days the players know each other and consider themselves friends. Whereas in the past, they didn't know each other and considered each other less than human (my words, not Coach's).

Maybe there is a lesson here. Maybe when we get to know our enemies, it's a lot harder to think of them as enemies. But I'm not sure it's a lesson I want to learn, because hating Hokes Bluff has always been so much fun.

~~~

The Hokes Bluff marching band began to play and their eagle mascot came in the room, and I swear it wouldn't stop staring it me. That evil bird could see into my soul, and if it could talk, it would have told the rest of the students that I was a spy.

There were skits and cheers, the team entered the room through smoke and dramatic music, and the goth kids hung out in the back, dreaming of the day they wouldn't have to go to this crap. Then some of the players stepped up to a microphone and informed the crowd that this was their house and people don't just walk into their house, although technically I had done just that. Finally I'd had just as much of a Hokes Bluff pep rally as I could take, so I snuck out the side door to beat traffic.

~~~

Coach Ozmint gave me permission to ride the Glencoe team bus to the game and even said I could join the team for the pre-game meal. At dinner I told Coach I'd been at the Hokes Bluff pep rally, and perhaps joking, perhaps looking for a little extra bulletin board material, he asked what had been said. But nothing had been said, apart from typical pep rally claims of not letting people walk into your house, so I said with a smile, "Coach, they said whatever you need them to have said."

After the meal, I walked through the locker room. The team was getting dressed and putting on eye black, most of them wearing headphones. The room felt nervous, and it made me nervous, which made me regret all the food I'd just inhaled. In the back, the coaches talked and joked a little, but even they seemed a bit on edge. Coach Ozmint walked out and gave a few logistical instructions to the team, then they watched Kenny Chesney's "The Boys of Fall" video on the projector screen. Finally, it was time to go.

They put me on the bus with the freshmen, who would likely not play tonight, along with the cheerleaders, who would also likely not play. Two of the cheerleaders actually told me they enjoyed my first book, but I didn't know what to say because talking to cheerleaders still makes me nervous. There wasn't a whole lot of talking on the bus, but even so, a coach popped his head in to remind the team that this was a business trip, and they needed to treat it as such. I didn't hear a word the rest of the way.

The buses pulled out of Yellow Jacket Stadium and turned down Lonesome Bend Road, passing stop signs with green "HB"s spray painted on them. A right on Highway 278, then a left on Appalachian Highway, and we were there. Even though it seemed like they were on different continents when I was growing up, the high schools are fewer than seven miles apart.

We pulled in to Eagles Stadium to the smell of burgers and hot dogs. Hokes Bluff was honoring the ten-year anniversary of their 2001 state championship team, and we saw the cookout across the stadium. The Glencoe team dropped off their equipment, then walked up and down the field, getting a feel for the turf, and I suppose inspecting for booby traps.

That 2001 Hokes Bluff team beat Glencoe 28–0, the Eagles' fifth straight victory over Glencoe. The streak stretched to eleven before Glencoe finally won, 14–7, at Hokes Bluff in 2008. The rivalry has been one of streaks, none longer than Glencoe's fourteen in a row from 1968 to 1981.

Love Thy Rival

It was on September 17, 1982, that Hokes Bluff came to Glencoe and ended that nearly a decade and a half of frustration with a 34–14 victory. The jubilant Eagles then drove the seven miles back to Hokes Bluff, turned on the lights to their stadium, posted 34-14 on the scoreboard, and partied on the field until early Saturday morning. Sam Griffith, who played on that Hokes Bluff team, told me a family friend thanked him with tears in his eyes, saying he never thought he'd see the day that Hokes Bluff beat Glencoe.

This is admittedly a charming story and may lead some of my unbiased readers to feel an affinity toward Hokes Bluff, but I implore you not to.

~~~

During warm-ups the stadium began to fill. I stood under the goal post, watching the players from both sides stretch and go through their pregame drills. For a second I shut my eyes and listened to the marching bands warming up outside the stadium, the little kids fighting behind the bleachers, the crack of shoulder pads crashing together, and the quick screech of a coach's whistle.

I saw Tricia and my parents walk through the gate, my dad hoping no one would recognize him from his days as an arsonist.

Back in the locker room the players joked around, trying to stay loose. Free safety Josh Jordan walked up to me and indicated he was going to intercept a pass in such a way I would have no choice but to write about it in my book. I just laughed and said we'd see. Then the coaches had everyone take a seat.

Offensive coordinator Brett Yancey spoke to his offense first. Brett and I were in school together, and he quarterbacked Glencoe to the state semifinals when I was a sophomore. A laid-back guy, Brett was pretty calm all day, but now he was screaming, probably trying to remind the team that even if they were friends with some Hokes Bluff kids, they were still the enemy. "I hate 'em!" Brett yelled. "And I want you to hate 'em too!" I nearly shouted amen.

Defensive coordinator Charlie Robertson, who came to Glencoe my fifth grade year, went over the defensive game plan, then stressed the importance of beating his brother, Hokes Bluff head coach Mike Robertson.

Then Coach Ozmint took center stage and asked us to shut our eyes, and moments later we were rushing out the door, but Hokes Bluff was still honoring their 2001 team, so the most fired up football team I've ever seen was told to wait. It would be a few minutes.

As we stood there, players bouncing on their toes, the room so full of energy I thought it might explode, I glanced over at Glencoe quarterback Harrison Bright, who raised his eyebrows and gave me the strangest smile. It was the look of someone who knew exactly how fortunate he was to be the starting quarterback for a team about to take the field against their archrival. I don't think I've ever been more jealous of someone in my life.

Someone shouted, "Let's go," and the door burst open again. The team went charging out, through the victory line, and onto the field. The Eagles came out through their own victory line, and we were ready for kickoff.

Glencoe struck fast, when Bright went deep down the sideline, hitting Austin Hancock for a sixty-nine-yard reception. Hancock was brought down at the Hokes Bluff three-yard line, and Bright ran it in from there to give Glencoe a 7–0 lead after only two minutes.

The Yellow Jacket defense held Hokes Bluff to a three and out on their first possession, then Glencoe marched fifty-five yards in ten plays for another score, this one a one-yard run by Daniel Otwell.

The teams traded possessions for the rest of the half, neither mounting much of a threat, until Bright hit Aaron Benefield in the back of the end zone just before halftime. The Yellow Jackets took a 20–0 lead to the locker room, the defense holding Hokes

Bluff to minus eight total yards in the first half.

The locker room buzzed with excitement, and I expected the coaches to come in and bring the team down to earth, but it was team leaders like linebacker Daniel Warren who wouldn't allow his teammates to let up, passionately reminding everyone there were two quarters left to play.

I watched the second half from the bleachers with Tricia and my folks. Glencoe ran clock, and Hokes Bluff, despite having a talented team led by running back Jacob Pennington, could never mount a threat. Late in the fourth quarter, Hokes Bluff attempted a pass over the middle, but Glencoe safety Josh Jordan, yes, that Josh Jordan, stepped in front of the receiver and tipped the ball high into the air. And as the Hokes Bluff receiver pulled him to the ground, Jordan reached out with one hand and pulled in one of the more spectacular interceptions I've ever seen. I turned to Tricia and said, "That kid told me he was going to do that and that I'd have to write about it."

"Well, I guess you'll have to write about it," she said.

Finally the horn sounded and the teams, coaches, and cheerleaders all met at midfield—shaking hands, hugging, and taking a knee for prayer. The locker room was equal parts blood, sweat, and celebration. I couldn't have been happier for the team, and I'm not sure I could have been more jealous of them either. Then the door opened behind me and some men helped Ed Ozmint into the room, where his son presented him with the game ball. There were few dry eyes.

~~~

The next day I went to see my cousin Jeff Little, whose son Brock was a junior on the Glencoe team. Jeff had some old Glencoe programs to show me. After I flipped through them he pointed out a framed shadowbox on his office wall. It contained the gold G from his father's Glencoe letterman jacket and the green HB from his mother's Hokes Bluff cheerleading sweater.

Jeff told me the reason he grew up in Southside (another rival of both Glencoe and Hokes Bluff, but that's another chapter for another book) was that his mom refused to live in Glencoe, while his dad refused to live in Hokes Bluff, so they split the difference.

The only big rivalries are our rivalries. I thought about that when I went around the country, seeing fans go insane over games I could not make myself care about. I thought about it again that Friday night in Hokes Bluff, when I was so excited about a game that only six or seven thousand people on earth care about. If we can take a step back and look at our rivals through a wide lens and know that 99 percent of the world could not care less, maybe then we can understand these games are just that: games. Because when you take away the artificial enormity, our games can be a lot of fun.[3]

---

3. This chapter is dedicated to my many dear friends from Hokes Bluff. Ruff the Bluff!

Army
vs.
Navy

FedEx Field – Landover, Maryland
December 10, 2011

I hate war as only a soldier who has lived it can.
—Dwight D. Eisenhower

"Do you guys hear a bugle?"

My friends Chris and Burns were just waking up, and I, having drawn the short straw for first shower, was getting dressed when we heard the sound of reveille echoing through our Washington, DC hotel parking lot. We grew quiet and listened until the last note was belted out, then gave each other impressed shrugs. It would be the first of many reminders that Army–Navy isn't just another rivalry.

Our hotel in Arlington was midway between the Pentagon and the Army and Navy Country Club (sorry Marines, no golf for you). Our room had views of the Dunkin' Donuts across the street, but before we checked out we rode the elevator to the top floor, where a ballroom overlooked our nation's capital. On the Virginia side, we could see the rows of white headstones at Arlington National Cemetery. Across the Potomac River, the Washington Monument dwarfed everything in sight.

Kickoff was set for 2:30, which gave us time to explore the National Mall. The day was cold and clear, and the three of us wore all the body-compressing Under Armour gear we could stand. We parked near the Washington Monument, which at the time of its completion was the tallest building in the world. It's still impressive, but the longer we stood and stared the colder we got.

We shivered past the WWII Memorial, and Chris said, "That doesn't look quite as nice in person." He was pointing to the reflecting pool, the one Forrest Gump hugged Jenny in, which was now more of a bubbling bog. A sign told us to forgive the progress, the pool was undergoing renovations and would be beautiful again sometime in the spring of 2012. We kept walking past the swamp, up the steps of the Lincoln Memorial, where Honest Abe sits atop his chair, looking out on the Mall, oblivious to the throngs of foreigners taking his photograph.

From there our walk continued. We took pictures of ourselves standing in front of the Korean War Memorial, which Chris's granddad fought in,[1] then the Vietnam War Memorial, then the MLK Memorial, and then we decided to drive over to the White House because we were freezing.

We parked next to Occupy DC's tent city and walked up toward President Obama's backyard. More protesters. The first group was against nuclear weapons. A sign read, "Ban all nuclear weapons or have a nice dooms day." Another large group asked the president to do more to stop dictators in the Middle East. An angry woman with a megaphone scolded Iraqi Prime Minister Nouri al-Malaki, chanting over and over, "Maliki, Maliki, shame on you, shame on you!" Chris and I chanted this for the rest of the trip, much to Burns' chagrin.

We stood outside the White House for a few minutes, but were not invited in. With half an hour to spare, we peeked inside the Smithsonian Museum of Natural History, where we saw the Hope Diamond and the bones of a *Tyrannosaurus rex*, before we left to watch Army and Navy play football for the 112th time.

---

1. The war, not the memorial.

~~~

The teams met for the first time in 1890, on the parade field at West Point. Navy won the game, 24–0. In Army's defense, it was their first ever football game, and only two of their players had even played before. Army won the second meeting, 32–16. By 1894, the rivalry had grown so intense that brawls broke out in the stands.[2] Embarrassed, President Grover Cleveland canceled the game; it resumed in 1899.

A Navy player from those early years and the future "father of carrier aviation," Joseph M. Reeves, is credited with being the first football player to wear a helmet. Navy doctors told Reeves that another blow to the head would result in "instant insanity" or death, so Reeves had a local shoemaker construct a leather helmet to protect his head.

By 1926, the Army–Navy game was so big that other coaches skipped their own games to see it. That year 7–1 Army played 9–0 Navy at Soldier Field in Chicago, and in attendance was Knute Rockne, head coach of the undefeated Notre Dame Fighting Irish, who were set to play lowly Carnegie Tech in Pittsburgh that day. Army and Navy tied, 21–21, while Notre Dame, without Rockne, was upset, 19–0. Navy went on to claim a share of the national championship.

Due to travel restrictions during WWII, the 1942 and 1943 games were played in Annapolis and West Point. At the 1942 game in Annapolis, under orders from the navy, a crew of midshipmen filled the visitor's section and cheered for Army. A year later a group of cadets returned the favor. I keep trying to envision a scenario in which Auburn students fill the visitor's section at Jordan-Hare to cheer for the Crimson Tide, but I can't.

From 1944–1946, Army was led by Doc Blanchard and Glenn Davis, aka Mr. Inside and Mr. Outside. Both Blanchard and Davis won the Heisman Trophy, in 1945 and 1946 respec-

---

2. There was also a near duel between a retired general and a rear admiral. A duel!

tively.[3] During their three years at West Point, the Black Knights went 27–0–1, winning the national championship each year. After the 1944 team beat Navy, General Douglas MacArthur cabled the winning locker room from the Philippines, saying, "We have stopped the war to celebrate your magnificent success."

Since the early 1960s the academies have faded from national championship contention. In the last fifty seasons, the Midshipmen have finished the season ranked only three times, Army just once. But the game remains popular with fans and is considered by many the finest tradition in American athletics. Major General Joe Robles wrote in this year's game program, "The Army–Navy game is the purest rivalry in college football, because these athletes are not playing for personal glory or future fame. They are patriots; brothers in the armed forces who play for a spirit of competition that is as American as the institutions they represent."

Americans tend to overdramatize sports. Our highlight videos are accompanied by classical music and breathy voiceovers, leading us to believe dunking a basketball is the most important thing a person could do in life. Army–Navy can sometimes go a little overboard on the sap-meter too, but they've earned it. The kids on the field are there because they've signed up to serve and protect our country, not because they were 5-star recruits looking for the surest path to NFL fame and riches. As an Army officer says in Showtime's documentary on Army–Navy called *A Game of Honor*, "Volunteering to attend West Point in a time of war is uniquely patriotic."

Since September 11, every young man and woman who signs on at West Point or Annapolis knows that in four years they will likely be going to war. This is uniquely patriotic, and in the occasionally scandal-plagued world of college football, it's a breath of fresh air. I'm usually annoyed when people talk about sports in

---

3. Pete Dawkins also won the Heisman Trophy for Army in 1958, while Joe Bellino and Roger Staubach both captured the award for Navy, in 1960 and 1963 respectively.

hyperbolic absolutes, but General Robles is probably right when he says Army–Navy is the purest rivalry in college football. This game deserves our attention.

~~~

Through the years, the game has been played all over the country, from Pasadena to New York, with most of the games taking place in Philadelphia. This year the Army–Navy game was played for the first time at FedEx Field in Washington, DC. Though if you want to get technical it was actually played in Landover, Maryland, home of, I suppose, the Landover Redskins. We hopped on the Capital Beltway and made our way over, fighting through the massive parking jam that surrounded the stadium.

I'm not sure what I expected to see at the game. I think somehow I'd convinced myself that everything would be as orderly as the Cadets and Midshipmen who march onto the field pregame.[4] That parking would be handled with military precision and tailgates would be organized like mess halls. Instead it looked like any other football game I'd ever seen. Parking was atrocious, RVs were wedged into every square inch of available blacktop, tents and chairs and grills and corn hole games were everywhere. And it seemed like every tailgate had a flagpole with old glory on top, an Army Black Knight or a Navy Goat just below.

A quick side story on mascots: Navy has had many live mascots over the years, including a cat, a bulldog, a carrier pigeon, and of course a gorilla. But since 1904, without interruption, a goat has served as the mascot. Apparently goats were always kept as pets on ships because (a) they ate the garbage and (b) they provided milk and butter.[5] Legend has it a navy vessel's pet goat died at sea, and the officers kept the skin to have it stuffed. Two ensigns were carrying the skin to the taxidermist when they

---

4. The Corps of Cadets and Brigade of Midshipmen march on much earlier than we'd thought, about three hours before kickoff. Needless to say, we missed it. Maybe next year.
5. Mmmm, garbage-eating goat butter.

decided to stop and watch a Navy game. During the game, one of the young officers dressed up as the deceased goat, much to the approval of the crowd. Navy won the game, and the goat became their mascot.

Army's official mascot is a mule, but the team is often referred to as the Black Knights of the Hudson, due to their black uniforms. Sure, that's not as interesting as Navy's story, but at least no one had to dress up in a dead animal carcass.

~~~

We walked through the parking lot, dodging footballs and growing hungrier at the smell of grilled burgers and brats. Near the stadium, waiting at will-call for our tickets, we saw our first West Point cadet. His face was that of a thirteen-year-old, and he had a 28-inch waist and the broad shoulders of someone who'd spent the last six semesters doing pushups. We were impressed and instinctively stood up straight and sucked in our guts, to no avail.

The cadets were dressed in their traditional gray uniforms, long gray coats with gold buttons over their gray uniforms, with a black and gray cap and what I guess you'd call a short gray cape. The midshipmen, who had equally youthful faces, small waists, and broad shoulders, wore their traditional black uniforms topped with a long black coat with gold buttons and a black and white cap. It almost made me wish Auburn had uniforms when I was in school, though I could do without the pushups.

We ventured inside the stadium a little early and joined the very long line at our gate. The line wasn't really moving though, and half an hour later we saw why. Each person had to walk though airport-style security and submit to a bit of a pat down. Turned out a rather important person would be flipping the coin to start the game.

We took our seats high in the upper deck of the west end zone and were immediately drawn to the video screen, which played spirit videos made by students or sent in from army and navy units serving around the world. One showed a couple of sailors sitting in a small boat in the middle of a desert, talking about how they can't wait to get out on the water. Then out of the blue a massive, tank-looking thing drives up and crushes the boat just as the sailors jump out. The Army officer driving the tank jumps out, stands over the sailors, and says the classic line from Jaws, "You're gonna need a bigger boat." A navy video showed a cadet lying on his bed crying while Sarah McLachlan's "Angel" played in the background, then went on to say Army was about to lose to Navy for the tenth straight time. The video ended by saying, "Hug a sad cadet today."

Most of the videos were hilarious—although some of the ones involving advanced weaponry were slightly intimidating—and all drew applause and laughter from the pregame crowd. After one of the funnier ones, I turned to Chris and Burns and said, "You know it's crazy, but we could never do this at the Alabama–Auburn game."

If students or alumni at Auburn or Alabama made a pregame video mocking the other team or school, it would be the scandal of the century in our state. Accusations of classlessness would abound, as would demands for public apologies. Student government leaders would be forced to step down in shame, and newspapers would print editorials citing the further decline of our once civil rivalry.

The Army–Navy rivalry is lauded as a shining example of what all rivalries should aspire to be. Gary Sinise, in his solemn narration of the 2011 Army–Navy game intro video on CBS, said, "This is truly a game of honor." When we talk of West Point and Annapolis, we use words like *courage*, *integrity*, and *character*. Yet here they are, making fun of each other.

It's not that Army and Navy don't take football seriously enough; they do. This game is a very big deal to everyone involved. But the key is they have a much better understanding of the importance of a game in the grand scheme of life. In

Alabama we could never joke about the Iron Bowl in this way because for most of us the game feels like it's life or death. For Army and Navy, the game is a break from the rest of their lives, which actually are life or death.

~~~

After the videos and before the coin toss, about a dozen midshipmen were led onto the field by a single cadet, where they were met by a single midshipmen leading about a dozen cadets. This was the annual prisoner exchange, where students who are spending the semester at their rival school as part of the Inter-Service Exchange Program are allowed to watch the game with their classmates. It was a very serious looking ceremony, until the nine midshipmen unfurled banners from their backs that spelled out "BEAT ARMY!" Both groups marched and then sprinted to their respective student sections to thunderous applause, many of them pulled up over the wall and into the welcoming arms of their classmates.

Then the Commander-in-Chief along with Vice President Biden were introduced to cheers from the eager crowd as they met the team captains at midfield for the coin toss. Navy took the field, running through a tunnel of fellow Midshipmen, a couple of their players carrying American flags. And as they entered the field, a squadron of F/A-18 Hornets buzzed the stadium and made me wish I'd spent more money on lower seats. Next Army took the field, marching slowly at first through a tunnel of fellow Cadets, then charging as a group of Apache helicopters flew over FedEx field. Outstanding!

Chris decided he would root for the Midshipmen, since his grandfather served in the Navy. Burns and I pulled for the Black Knights, because his grandfather and my father both served in the Army.[6] The game started slow, although the clock moved fast, because these teams do not like to throw the ball—their

---

6. Burns quickly made friends with all the Army fans around us by making loud and slightly inappropriate seamen jokes.

reluctance to go to the air perhaps stemming from their mutual hatred of the Air Force Academy. The teams combined for nine total passes, Army completing four, Navy just one.

Finally, with just over a minute to play in the first quarter, Navy got on the scoreboard when quarterback Kriss Proctor ran in from three yards out. Midway through the second quarter, Navy scored again, this time on a ten-yard run from senior fullback Alexander Teich. It was 14–0 Navy, and a tenth straight win looked inevitable.

But Army answered, marching slowly down the field, and when quarterback Trent Steelman broke off a thirty-four-yard touchdown run, the Navy lead was cut in half. Army held Navy on their following possession, then, miracle of miracles, completed a ten-yard pass en route to a sixty-three-yard scoring drive capped by a five-yard Malcolm Brown run. It was 14–14 at the half. We had ourselves a ballgame.

At halftime a line of cadets and midshipmen formed a human tunnel at midfield, and President Obama walked through, officially switching sides for the second half, from Navy to Army. After the US Naval Academy Drum and Bugle Corps performed, Lee Greenwood took the field to sing, you guessed it, "I'm Proud to Be an American," while a massive American flag unfurled on the field. This surpassed opening day at Fenway as the most patriotic moment of my life.[7]

Navy opened the second half scoring with a two-yard touchdown run from Kriss Proctor, but again Army answered with something no one was expecting, a twenty-five-yard touchdown pass from Steelman to Brown.

Tied at 21 going into the fourth quarter, Navy kicker Jon Teague added two field goals early on to give the Midshipmen a six-point lead. But six-point leads are never safe, ever, and fans on both sides sensed it. With ten tense minutes to play, Army took possession and drove the ball down to the Navy twenty-five-yard

---

7. USA! USA! USA!

line, but they would get no closer as Steelman lost yardage on a fourth and seven play.

Navy took possession and milked the clock, a tenth straight victory almost in their grasp. The Army defense stiffened, and on fourth and one at midfield, with just over two minutes to play, Navy lined up to go for it. As Navy quarterback Kriss Proctor barked out the signals, an Army defender jumped off-sides, giving Navy a first down, all but ending the game. Army took possession on their own goal line with a handful of seconds to play, but the clock ran out after a final completion, and Navy beat Army.[8]

The Midshipmen celebrated on the field while their classmates went ballistic in the stands. There were handshakes and hugs, and then the Black Knights made the slow walk down to the corner of the stadium where their fellow cadets stood to applaud their effort. The PA announcer asked for everyone to please rise for the playing of the United States Military Academy's alma mater. And with the rival Midshipmen standing respectfully behind them, the Army team and their fellow cadets sang, belting out "Beat Navy!" after the final note.

Then came a roar of noise from the Navy section as the Midshipmen dashed across the end zone to stand victorious in front of their fellow students. And with the Black Knights now standing respectfully behind them, the Midshipmen sang "Navy Blue and Gold," belting out "Beat Army!" after the last note.

As the teams started to leave the field, the PA announcer said, "Attention all midshipmen: The Commandant of the Midshipmen has granted an uncharged overnight for all midshipmen. Furthermore, the class of 2015 is granted carryon until Christmas." I had no idea what any of that meant, but based on the roar of approval from the midshipmen, it must be a good thing.

~~~

---

8. Navy leads the all-time series, 56–49–7, which means when their current streak began, it was Army who led the all-time series by two games.

A few weeks later, my year of traveling to rivalry games over, Tricia asked which trip had been my favorite. I told her that seeing Duke vs. Carolina at Cameron Indoor had been a dream come true, and the insane passion at Celtic vs. Rangers in Glasgow was something I will never forget, but if I had to pick my favorite rivalry game, it would be Army vs. Navy.

Army vs. Navy gets it right. The game has all the passion and pageantry of the Iron Bowl, or The Game, or the Red River Shootout. BCS Bowl berths may not be up for grabs, but you'd never know it sitting in the stands. For three hours in December, nothing matters more than beating Army or beating Navy. But then the game ends, and you see the respect both sides have for each other. It seems the commitment the Cadets and Midshipmen have made to their country give a perfect balance to the rivalry. When life gets too serious and the realities of war too real, the game is a most welcome distraction. When the game becomes too big, and when fans want to make the game bigger than it is, the commitment of the players and reality of war remind everyone what is truly important.

I spoke to Chet Moeller, a Navy defensive back from the mid seventies and member of the College Football Hall of Fame, and he said the rivalry is a little different because, "As soon as you graduate, you are working together. It gets a little intense, but it's all in fun. You act like you hate the other team when you are there, but you obviously don't hate them." He went on to say that a lot of the respect comes from players on both sides being the same type of athlete, going through the same things at their respective academies.

It's the respect the academies show toward one another that moved me. Don't get me wrong, when an Iron Bowl ends, the players hug and shake hands and show a great deal of respect as well, but in the stands we tend to forget it's a game. When Alabama beats Auburn, the crowd sings "Rammer Jammer," letting Auburn know the Tide just beat the hell out of them. When Auburn beats Alabama, the song is reversed. How awkward would that be for Navy fans to sing, when the Army players are respectfully lining up for their rival's alma mater?

I've got nothing against "Rammer Jammer" or trash talking or any of that. Army and Navy certainly did a great deal of trash talking before the game via spirit videos. And I found some Army and Navy message boards, and even they have crazy fans who take things too far. What bothers me is when we forget that Auburn–Alabama or Duke–Carolina or any other rivalry game is just that. A game.

I asked my friend Billy Wilson, who played football at West Point for two years before leaving to pursue the ministry, about this, and he quoted the great line from General Douglas MacArthur, "On the fields of friendly strife are sown the seeds that on other days and other fields will bear the fruits of victory."

It's obvious what this quote means to a young man or woman at West Point or Annapolis. The game is important, but in light of their greater calling, it is only a game.

I love sports. I really do. I love screaming for my team until I lose my voice, and I love getting nervous for no good reason. I'm starting to even appreciate the kick in the stomach you feel after a tough loss. But just like the cadets and midshipmen, I have a higher calling than sports. As a Christian, I believe I have the highest calling, as do many of my brothers and sisters in Christ who cheer for my rivals. And just like Army and Navy, when the game is over, we have to work together. No matter what happens on the field or in the stands, that is something we need never to forget.

A Time to Love

Alabama
vs.
Auburn

Jordan-Hare Stadium – Auburn, Alabama
November 26, 2011

Hate is too great a burden to bear.
—Martin Luther King Jr.

2011 was an interesting year to live in Alabama, and it was a particularly interesting year to write a book about hate in sports rivalries. As I've mentioned, in the weeks following the 2010 Iron Bowl (the one I couldn't sleep before at the beginning of this book), a troubled man by the name of Harvey Updyke Jr. drove to Auburn with enough poison to kill every living thing in Yellowstone National Park, and he dumped it all on the two oak trees that make up Toomer's Corner,[1] the trees Auburn fans have been rolling for years to celebrate anything they thought needed celebrating.

When Updyke called the Paul Finebaum radio show in January to brag about what he'd done, he claimed his act was in retaliation for Auburn fans rolling the trees the day legendary Alabama coach Paul "Bear" Bryant died. Whether or not this happened I cannot say—I was five at the time—but I have never seen any evidence, photographic or otherwise, to suggest Auburn fans were out reveling in the death of an old man who had already retired. But let's assume for a moment a couple of idiotic

1. Allegedly, and sometimes admittedly.

Auburn students did go out and throw toilet paper in the trees: Why did Updyke feel the need to avenge this slight to his beloved coach thirty years after the fact?

I think the answer lies in an interview Updyke gave during *Roll Tide/War Eagle*, an ESPN documentary produced to show just how out of hand the Auburn–Alabama rivalry had gotten—that's right, things got so crazy last year people were making documentaries about us. As Updyke explains himself, he makes parallels to Tommy Lewis, an Alabama player who charged off the bench during the 1954 Cotton Bowl to tackle a Rice player before he scored yet another touchdown. When asked later why he did it, Lewis replied that he had too much Bama in him. Updyke says the same thing about himself, then looks straight into the camera and says, "I don't have my priorities straight."

Yeah, no kidding Harvey. It's not hard to realize you have priority issues when you're being charged with a class-C felony. But what about when passion for sports causes us to act in ways that aren't illegal, but certainly aren't bringing glory and honor to God? At least Harvey is aware his priorities are off. Am I? Are you?

~~~

In January, as I started work on this book, I visited the headquarters of the publishing house that published my first book. I had dinner with some editors and marketing folks, and eventually talk turned to football. "I've watched last year's Iron Bowl at least thirty times already," I confessed during appetizers. They thought I was joking, since barely a month had passed since the game. I assured them I was not. "I mean, I haven't just turned it on and watched it straight through thirty times, but if I'm at home working, I'll turn it on and let it play in the background." The people sitting next to me discretely pushed their chairs a few inches away, positive they were dining with a lunatic, then I confirmed their suspicions. "And here's the crazy thing: I'm getting to the point where I enjoy watching the first half more than the second."

"Wait," said one of the men who remembered Auburn's dramatic comeback win. "You enjoy watching the parts where Alabama scored?"

"I do," I confessed. "I like watching the players and fans get excited, knowing how miserable they will be when the game ends."

Everyone looked at me like I said I enjoyed looking at the humane society's website because I knew the kittens would soon be put down. They thought I was crazy, and in their defense, this stupid rivalry does make me crazy. It makes all of us crazy.

During the year, I conducted a survey asking fans about their rivals. I heard from hundreds of people, and here is a short sample of Auburn and Alabama fans talking about each other:

"I have no respect for them."

"There are few things in this world I truly hate, and they are one of them."

"Sometimes it's real hate. I know I need to let it go, but I do get really angry."

"People from church tell me all the time that the rivalry turns me into a jerk."

"Sometimes I wish terrible things like death or at least terrible pain on them, and while I say I'm joking, I sometimes wonder if I really am."

"I don't really even consider them people."

"They were the first thing I learned to hate."

"I honestly cannot think of anyone or anything else that I truly hate the way I hate them."

"Yes, I hate them. I truly hate them. When I see someone walking down the street wearing those colors, I instantly hate them. And I'm a kind person; I feel that loving your neighbor is one of the more important things in life."

"I hate them, not any one individual, just the idea of

them."

"It's hate. I've tried to get myself out of that mode of thinking, but I honestly just hate them."

"Yes, I use the word *hate*, and I fully mean it."

"I hate them and wouldn't cheer for them if my life depended on it."

"I use the word *hate* and do so correctly."

"Yes, I hate them, and not just in sports either."

"I usually don't say 'hate.' I usually say 'abhor' or 'subhuman.' It isn't a joke."

What is wrong with us? I think Chris Hahn, the pastor from Southland Christian in Lexington, nailed it. "Honestly," he told me, "I think it stems from idolatry. When we put our team on the throne in the middle of our lives, which a lot of us tend to do, that's when perspective gets skewed. And hatred does naturally flow out toward something that crosses what you idolize."

I'm friends with Lee Webb, an Auburn alum and news anchor on CBN and the *700 Club*. We spoke a few days after the 2011 season ended, and Lee told me about an incident that occurred all the way back during Auburn's first game of the season against Utah State.

"I thought Auburn winning that national championship had maybe satisfied the sports fan in me," Lee said. "But we opened the season against Utah State, and it looked like they were going to knock us off. I remember seeing their coach on the sideline, celebrating the apparent victory, and all of a sudden I was just filled with hatred for that man. Of course Auburn came back and won, but when my wife got home I told her I have to take a break from this stuff. The next Saturday I not only fasted from football, but I fasted from food, and spent the time that Auburn was playing Mississippi State alone in prayer, asking God to rid my life of this idolatry. It was not easy, but I believe God is faithful in rooting out sin in our lives."

I know exactly what Lee is talking about because I was at that game, and for a brief time, I hated the Utah State fans in front of us for celebrating their apparent victory. Why? Because at times Auburn football is still an idol in my life. Not always, and since I wrote God and Football, I'm better. But still, I slip, and Chris Hahn was right, when something crosses our idol, we naturally hate it. And it's our rival who crosses our idol on a daily basis. We hate our rivals because we know they relish in our failure. It's symbiotic; we need each other to be happy, but our happiness comes only at each other's misfortune. If I look at my team as a group of athletes assembled for the sole purpose of bringing me happiness, then our rival team has been assembled for the sole purpose of bringing me pain. Anyone who cheers for that team is cheering for my misery. It's not hard to hate someone if you think they are cheering for your misery.

~~~

It takes a lot for people in Alabama to stop talking about football. September 11 almost did, though I still have a sneaking suspicion that we would have played football the following Saturday if we didn't think the rest of the nation would give us dirty looks. It takes a lot to get our minds off football, but a 1.5-mile-wide tornado will do the trick.

I sat on my couch in Auburn on April 27, 2011, watching on television as a massive tornado ripped through Tuscaloosa. On my laptop I kept refreshing Twitter, looking for tweets from friends, praying they were okay. They were, though one frantically tried to find his parents, another reported that DCH Regional Medical Center had been destroyed, and another said Tuscaloosa looked like it had been bombed.

Two hundred thirty-five people died in Alabama that day, forty-four in Tuscaloosa alone. Football, for once, was the furthest thing from our minds. Even the Paul Finebaum show, which is typically a 50,000-watt megaphone for the craziest fans in the state, took a break from football talk to mourn and reflect on the tragic events.[2]

Many people told me they think what makes our rivalry so great is also what makes it so terrible. We know each other. We work with each other, we are related to each other, we marry each other.[3] We are like brothers who have to share bunk beds in a tiny bedroom. We can't get away from each other, ever. But I think we hate the way brothers hate, and when something happens to one, the other will be there to help. We saw it in the Alabama response to Updyke's oak tree massacre. An organization called Tide for Toomer's was formed, and Alabama fans sent money to Auburn to help save or one day replace the trees. And just after the tornados of April 27, Toomer's for Tuscaloosa was formed, sending money, supplies, and volunteers to Tuscaloosa to assist in cleanup and recovery. We still have the capacity to put things in perspective and do the right thing, but usually our motive is to get things back to normal as quickly as possible, so we can start hating each other again. As Finebaum said in the ESPN documentary, "For the most part for a couple of weeks it stayed pretty sane, but then it was like the tornado had never happened."

~~~

I slept like a baby the night before the 2011 Iron Bowl. Compared with the night before the 2010 game, when I tossed and turned well past the witching hour, I felt that was quite an accomplishment. I had no illusions that Auburn would upset the #2-ranked Crimson Tide the next day, and any dread I had of losing to our rival had slowly turned to acceptance. I was sleeping and was convinced life would indeed go on no matter what happened on Saturday afternoon.

We had an extra pair of tickets to the game, and to prove I

2. If you are reading this book from another part of the country and you are not familiar with the Auburn–Alabama rivalry, you may think, "Well, of course you wouldn't be talking about football in April." But we do talk football in April. And in May, and in July, and on Christmas Day, and at church, and at funerals…

3. No we don't marry the ones we are related to. Shut up!

wasn't consumed with hate, I gave them to my parents. My dad is an Auburn fan, but my mom is such a Bama fan she wrote "Roll Tide" on every tuition check she ever mailed to Auburn. If I could sit by Mom through an Iron Bowl that Auburn was likely to lose, I could do anything.

We walked from our house to the game, making our way through campus to Jordan-Hare Stadium. The scene was exactly as I'd expected. Auburn fans tailgating and having a nice time. Alabama fans tailgating and having a nice time. Many of the Auburn and Alabama fans were tailgating together, and no one was fighting, or cursing, or shooting crossbows in the other's direction. There had been so much talk during the year that our rivalry was out of control, as if fans from each school could not look at each other without pulling a knife, that I figured campus would look like the Thunderdome that afternoon. It did not.

Perhaps I'm in the minority, but I think our rivalry is okay. Sure there are crazies on both sides, and if you listen to call-in shows all day you might get the impression our entire state should be locked in a padded cell. But it's not a violent rivalry. I've never feared for my safety at an Iron Bowl. And I don't think we hate each other, not really. When the tornado struck Tuscaloosa, Auburn fans didn't set up barricades on the interstate to stop relief trucks from getting to those in need. That would be real hate.

Our problem is we idolize our teams, and we order our lives around our teams and look for our happiness and our identity in our teams. We dislike our rival, not because they exist, but because they exist to defeat our team.

Mom and I didn't fight during the game, although her insistence on grabbing my arm while celebrating big plays for the Tide tested me. After three AJ McCarron touchdown passes, Alabama led 24–7 at the half, the exact score from a year before, a coincidence that failed to get my hopes up for the second half. Onterio McCalebb's eighty-three-yard touchdown return of the second half kickoff did raise my hopes for a second, but a Dee Milliner interception return for a score to start the forth quarter all but sealed the deal.

Our season tickets were right next to the visitor's section, and since the first game we'd talked about how there were probably better places to watch the Iron Bowl, like Beirut. But it wasn't that bad. It really wasn't. And my mom had the time of her life, and I'm very thankful I was able to give her the ticket. We even posed for a photograph together late in the game, her holding up the #1 finger, me crying. But as the final seconds ticked down, and Alabama's Million Dollar Band began warming up for "Rammer Jammer," I turned to Mom and said, "I trust you can find your way back to our house."

"You're not staying for the celebration?" she asked in mock disbelief.

"I love you, Mom, but not that much."

Epilogue

I met again with my former pastor Al Jackson after the season, and we talked about sports and fanhood, and Bro Al asked me some pretty tough questions. Questions he said all Christian sports fan need to ask themselves.

"Does your devotion to sports glorify God?" he asked. "It should, and if it doesn't, it's sin."

I wondered what sports fanaticism that glorifies God even looks like. Perhaps losing graciously. Or winning with humility. Keeping banter friendly and treating rival fans the way I want to be treated. Certainly not taunting others and grieving losses the way I would grieve my grandmother.

Recently I've begun looking at decisions I make in a different way. Not asking, "What would Jesus do?" but asking, "How would I explain this to Jesus?" Say Jesus went with me to the Iron Bowl, and on the drive home he said, "So tell me again why you were telling Alabama fans to go to hell."

"Well you see, Jesus, it's this cheer, and, uh, well…. Hey, what do you think about that new Rob Bell book?"

Brother Al continued, "What about others? Does your devotion to sports cause others to stumble?"

When I think of causing others to stumble, I usually think of gambling or drinking, and how some recovering alcoholic or degenerate gambler may see me having a glass of wine while playing a penny slot machine and just go over the edge. I don't think I've ever thought of my devotion to sports as something that could cause others to stumble, but then I thought about Facebook.

You've done it. I've done it. We've all posted things online that we know will stir up opposing fans. And sure, if you let some comment on Facebook push you into a rage, you probably need to step back and reexamine your devotion to your team. But if I post something because I know it's going to make people mad and start some thread that will quickly devolve into name calling or worse, then I'm being a jerk. Don't be a jerk.

"Finally," Bro Al asked, "do you use sports as a counter cultural witness? Does your devotion to sports assist you in proclaiming the gospel of salvation?"

Wait, what? I've always thought things like sports were just supposed to not interfere with my witness. That I was supposed to balance my hobbies and interests with my faith, to make sure that the former doesn't intrude on the latter. Now I'm being asked how my sports fanaticism is assisting in proclaiming the gospel. How would that even work?

~~~

Brother Al's final question bothered me for weeks until I reread the gospel of Luke. A religious leader asked Jesus what he must do to inherit eternal life. Jesus asked in return what was written in the law. The religious leader said to love God with all your heart, soul, and strength, and to love your neighbor as yourself. "Correct," Jesus said. "Do it and you will live." But the leader pressed further and asked Jesus, "But who is my neighbor?"

Jesus goes on to tell what we call the parable of the good Samaritan, a story of a Jewish traveler beaten and left for dead by a gang of robbers. A priest walks by and doesn't help, then a Levite does the same, but finally a Samaritan sees the man, takes pity on him, and nurses him back to health.

The story was shocking to a first-century Jew because a Samaritan was not someone they associated with "good," unless it was followed closely by "for nothing." When this religious leader asked Jesus who his neighbor was, Jesus showed him a perceived enemy.

You notice no one ever asked Jesus, "Who is my enemy?" We think we know who our enemies are. They are the people with different political agendas than ours, people with different religious views than ours, and sometimes people who cheer for different teams than ours.

But those are not our enemies. Alabama fans are not my enemy. Duke fans, Yankees fans, Oklahoma fans are not yours. Whether they wear purple and gold, crimson and cream, or maize and blue, they are oftentimes our brothers and sisters in Christ. They are always our neighbors.

We have a common enemy; it's called sin. Until it is ultimately defeated it's up to us to battle with its offspring; sickness, helplessness, and despair.

How can we use our sports fanaticism as a countercultural witness? I suppose we have to look at sports culture and act counter to that. Sports culture says rival fans are enemies. It says that we hate each other, and if Satan and his minions were playing our rival in an exhibition, we'd show up at the game carrying a pitchfork. That's why I think the most countercultural thing we can do is partner with our rivals to bring glory to God. Join forces and feed the hungry, heal the sick, and comfort those in despair. And when someone asks why these hated rivals have joined forces, we can say because we love God more than we love our team, and we hate sin more than we hate our rival.

What's that? You're convicted and inspired and looking for an opportunity to use your sports fanaticism to bring glory to God? Then please visit…

www.chadgibbs.com/samaritanspurse

or

www.firstgiving.com/fundraiser/chadgibbs/lovethyrival

…and learn how rival fans and Samaritan's Purse have teamed up to do God's work in Haiti.

Samaritan's Purse®
INTERNATIONAL RELIEF

Five Others

While this book preaches a healthier perspective on sports, it is not an anti-sports book. Not even close. I had a blast traveling around the country watching these epic rivalry games. My only regret is I couldn't see more of them. So real quick like, here are five more rivalry games I wish I could have seen.

1. Ouachita Baptist University vs. Henderson State University (Football) – My friends Chris Babb and Rex Nelson invited me half a dozen times to witness the Battle of the Ravine, but unfortunately I couldn't make it in 2011. The oldest football rivalry in Division II, Henderson State now leads the unbelievably tight all-time series 40-39-6. However the most intriguing aspect of the rivalry is that the schools are literally across the street from one another, and on game day the visitors just walk from their own locker room across Highway 7 to their rival's stadium, hopefully stopping to look both ways.

2. State of Origin (Rugby) – The Australian kid we sat next to in Glasgow the night before Celtic-Rangers, when not talking about the Illuminati, kept insisting that State of Origin was the greatest spectacle in sports. And while I generally do not trust people who are that concerned with vast global conspiracies, I checked and many consider State of Origin the greatest rivalry in rugby. The three match series is played annually between Queensland and New South Wales in Australia. The players represent the state from which they first played senior rugby league. I guess it's sort of like the North and South teams at the Senior Bowl in Mobile, but not really. Queensland leads the all-time series 20-12-2.

3. St. Johns College vs. The United States Naval Academy (Croquet) – The legend says sometime in the early 1980's, in a barroom no doubt, a Midshipman challenged a St. Johns student, saying Navy could beat St. Johns at any sport. St. Johns chose croquet. Now every year thousands of spectators come out to watch the match on the front lawn of St. Johns, dressed in their Gatsby-era finest. GQ has called the match, "the purest intercollegiate athletic event in America." St. Johns leads the all-time series 25-5, which is why their fight song ends with the lines, "O hear us when we boldly say, Defeat the middies at croquet!"

4. India vs. Pakistan (Cricket) – Wright Thompson, who covered the 2011 Cricket World Cup for ESPN, once tried to explain the game to me, but it still makes no sense. Even so, I love an intense rivalry, and India vs. Pakistan is perhaps the most intense of them all. When these two counties play, an estimated 300 million viewers tune in, though from time to time the two countries will stop playing cricket so they can wage actual wars against each other. I'm pretty sure Pakistan leads the all-time series, but don't quote me.

5. Gryffindor vs. Slytherin (Quidditch) - A rivalry that goes all the way back to the era of Godric Gryffindor and Salazar Slytherian, the all-time record is not known to Muggles, though we do know that Gryffindor defeated Slytherin during Harry Potter's 1st, 2nd, 3rd, 5th, and 6th years at Hogwarts. Weasley Is Our King!

You know what? I'd like to see Barcelona vs. Madrid, UCONN vs. Tennessee, Giants vs. Dodgers, Nadal vs. Federer, The Ryder Cup, USC vs. Notre Dame, Manchester United vs. Manchester City, Oregon vs. Oregon State, Flyers vs. Penguins, Florida vs. Georgia, Lafayette vs. Lehigh, South Carolina vs. Clemson, Ali vs. Frazier, Seabiscuit vs. War Admiral, Man vs. Food, Hatfields vs. McCoys, Chi Omega vs. Kappa Delta, Hamilton vs. Burr, water vs. oil, and few dozen others. Maybe I should just write another book.

Acknowledgements

Thanks to my wife, Tricia. Every word I write is for you.

Thanks to my parents, Kim and Alan Gibbs, for teaching me not to play with fire, unless I'm in Hokes Bluff.

Thanks to Brian Brown who designed this book, cover to cover, for the amazingly low prices of zero dollars. I hope you'll at least let me buy you lunch.

If this were the Academy Awards they'd now be playing music and telling me to wrap it up. But this is my book, and I can do whatever I want. I can put a question mark at the end of a declarative sentence? I can spell my last name with a dollar sign; Gibb$. And I can thank all of my friends and family who have given me such tremendous support through the years...

Amy and Craig Aarhus, Erica, Bryan, Kylie & Parker Allain, Sam Allison, Ricky Anderson, Ashleigh, Beau, Garrett, Morgan and Chandler Ashley, Chris Babb, Clark Bailey, Mary Baird, Codi and Landon Ball, Amanda Bast & The Joseph Craven, Mark Bast, Amber and Jason Battles, Shay and Marc Baugh, Kristin and JT Berney, Ann and Pat Bethea, Sarah Grace and Patrick Beverly, Keith Blackwood, Andy Blauser, Lyn Blount, Allison and Zac Boman, Jason Boyett, Kyle Bradberry, Meg and Kurt Branch, Nicole Brockhouse, Haley Brown, Ryan Brown, Ann and John Bryant, Lori and Jeremy Burns, Melanie and Kevin Burson, Jessica Buttram, Lacey and Lee Cadden, Jason Caldwell, Scott Calhoun and Hokes Bluff High School, Lando Calrissian, Hillary and Justin Campbell, Stacey and

Kevin Carden, Debbie Carper, James Cartee, Larry Carter, Lori and Chris Cate, Sarah Catt, Matt Chenoweth, Jesus Christ, Alicia and Russell Clayton, Clinton School of Public Service, Ross Collings, Tor Constantino, Sarah and Jason Cook, Keith Cooke, Kathryn Corey, Rick Cornutt, Tripp Cosby, Anna and Ryan Cothran, Brett Cowden, Hilary and Phillip Coxwell, Gary D'Amato, Evy Dandurand, Phyllis and Tom Davis, Ken Davis, Rachel Davis, Sally and Nick Davis, Karen and Harrell Day, Leita and Dawson Day, Drew Deener, Amanda and Rees Denham, Nikolai DiPippa, Aaron Donley, Lori, Johnny, Ava, and Jake Dorminey, Alisah Duran, Rich Edmondson, Drew Espy, Rachel Held Evans, John Ferguson, Cheryl Fletcher, Robin and Tommy Ford, Mariska and Billy Frey, Natalie and Adam Fulgham, Jody Gambrell, Leslianna and Andy Garlington, Maury Gaston, Don Gates, Sam and George Gibbs, Randee, Kelly, and Nathan Gibbs, Jaclyn and David Gibbs, Charlton Giles and Glencoe High School, Bryan Gill, Austin Gilly, Jeff Goins, Jamie Golden, Marcus Goodloe, Mindy and Jordan Green, Vick Green, Amanda and Benji Green, Jason Gregg, Amy and Sam Griffith, Katy Haber, Stephen Haggerty, Kevin Haggerty, Chris Hahn, Matt Haines, Brad Haines, Tara and Jason Harbison, Flint Harris, Gina and Brian Harris, Leslie and Chris Harrison, Catherine Hartman, Jenny and Kelly Heegard, Amanda and Michael Helms, Kelly and Heath Henderson, Laurel Hendrix, Staci and Daniel Henson, Kathryn and Rusty Herring, Robert Hogeland, Justin Hokanson, Kelly Holderman, Jared Hollier, Todd Hollinghead, April and Jonathan Hollingsworth, Adam Hollingsworth, Whitney and JT Hornbuckle, Lynne and Brandon Howard, Natalie and Kevin Humphrey, Rusty Hutson and our church family at Cornerstone in Auburn, Susan Isaacs, Bethany and Billy Ivey, Mandy and Ryan Johnson, Hunter Swagger Johnson, Brian Johnson, Chad Jones, Craig Jordan, Philip Justiss, Linda Kay, Angie and Grahl Keener, Adam Kidd, Marc Kostic, Leigh Kramer, Kate Larkin, Wormy and Hays Latimer, Jeffrey Lee, Leslie, Jeff, Baileigh, Brock, and Breia Little, Keat Liton, JD Lloyd, Bob Lochamy, Jenny and Matt Loving, Paul Loyless, Tamara Lunardo, Chip MacGregor, Traci and Charles Marsh, Chris Mason, Bryan Matthews, Stu McAllister, Leigha and John McClendon, Knox McCoy, Carolyn McCready, Jeanette and Benny McDonald, Sara and Jay McFarland, Caleb McNary, Mandy McPherson, Leanne and Matt McWilliams, Laura and Bo Megginson, Mandy and Andy Meisenheimer, Jacque and Jonathan Middleton, Laura and Nick Mielke, Brooke and Josh Miller, Mary Leah and The Rodney Miller, Tipi and Wes Miller, Sally and Napo Monasterio, Mark Moody, Tammy, Jim, Logan and Lauren Moore, Brian Moore, Alex Morando, Molly and Bo Morrissey, Rob Moxley, Ryan Mudd, Scott Murchsion, Justin "J-Murph" Murphy, Tony Neely, Rex Nelson, Kate Neilsen and my friends at Community Foundation of Greater Birmingham, Rex Nelson, Jeni and Chad Newbolt, Stephanie Nikolopoulos, Cody O'Brien, Naomi and Matt O'Reilly, Sherri Parrish Oden, Lee Ozmint and the Glencoe High School coaching staff, Richard Johnson (Secondary), Jason Gilley (Defensive Ends), Chris Sanders (Running Backs), Skylar Deerman (Recievers), Ryan Barkley (Linebackers), Wes Weems (Defensive Line), Will Hill (Offensive Line), Christine & David Palmer, Jill Parrish, Cindy and Mark Parrish, Stephen Parrish, Barbara and Benny Parrish, Heather Parrish, Deena and Jim Parrish, Michael Perkins, Ashleigh and John Perritt, Sandy and Matt Phelps, Becky and Matt Philpott, Melissa and Adam Pierce, Robert Pitman, Ashley and Kyle Powell, Hannah and Randy Presley, Lauren and Nick Rachel, Thom Rainer, Jake Reiss and The Alabama Booksmith, Marcia and Wayne Rhodes, Rick and Bubba, Sam Rives, Drew Roberts, Tara and Scott Robinson, Gary Robinson, Megan Roggendorff, Jordan Ross, Emily and Hugh Rushing, Skip Rutherford, Brittany and Charlie Saliba, Andrew Salser, Amanda & Jonathan Savage, Jimmy Scott, Angela Scheff, Larry Shallenberger, David Shaul,

Love Thy Rival

Ben Shell, Rob Shepherd, John Sherman, Ari and David Shirk, Leanne Shirtliffe, Lisa and Jarrod Simmons, Ric Smith, Jerry Smith, Shawn Smucker, Stacey and Billy Solomon, SOOF, The Sports Czars, Tracy, Tommy, Kaci and Lexie Stanley, Tyler Stanton, Rob Stennett, Erin and Scott Stephenson, Scott Stevenson, Judy and Steve Stocks, Dave Stone, Lisa and Michael Strane, Allen Sullivan, Jonathan Sutton, Tyler and Juno Tarver, Jarrett Tate, @thejuiceisgood, These Numbers Have Faces, Tiger Rags, Beth and Scott Tindle, Robby Townes, Tripp Vickers, Matthew Paul Turner, Patrick Tyndall, Griff Tyndall, Tasha and Curtis Tyus, David Van Horn, HARPER! and Bob Vance, Eric Wade, Volree and Nick Wade, Lindsey and Bruce Walsh, Lee Webb, Lauren and Kevin Webb, Amy and Patrick White, Karen and Roger Wiggins, Kelly and Adam Williams, Sarah and Billy Wilson, Dawn Wingard, Rachel Winter, Susan and Nick Wintermantel, WJOX Round Table, Alise Write, Karen Zacharias, Trisha and Justin Zoradi, and finally thanks to all the readers, book sellers, libraries, churches, and civic groups for giving me the best job in the world.

Of course the problem with thanking this many people is that I've undoubtedly forgot someone, and for this I offer a Madlib apology.

I am truly sorry I left _Your Name_ out of the acknowledgements. I hope they will _Verb_ me, and still buy _Your Age_ copies of my _Noun_ as Christmas presents.

And now a list of thirty blogger friends who agreed to promote the Samaritan's Purse - Haiti campaign.

www.shawnsmucker.com
www.badlydrawnbible.com
www.meetthebuttrams.com
www.mandiemarie.com
www.goinswriter.com
www.clay-morgan.com
www.knoxmccoy.com
www.tamaraoutloud.com
www.alise-write.com
www.ironicmom.com
www.thegboat.net
www.jamiesrabbits.com
www.calebmcnary.com
www.isleofman.net
www.thebeardedidealist.com
www.austingilly.wordpress.com
www.randomlychad.com
www.bryanallain.com
www.tylerstanton.com
www.robshep.com
www.rickyanderson.net
www.thedailyretort.com
www.justinzoradi.com
www.warblogle.com
www.friendsoftheprogram.com
www.deuceology.wordpress.com
www.saturdaydownsouth.com
www.holyturf.com
www.leighkramer.com
www.larryshallenberger.com

Select Bibliography

Bissinger, Buzz. "NBA All-Star Game: White Men Can't Root." The Daily Beast. Newsweek/Daily Beast, 17 Feb. 2011. Web.

Blythe, Will. To Hate like This Is to Be Happy Forever: A Thoroughly Obsessive, Intermittently Uplifting and Occasionally Unbiased Account of the Duke-North Carolina Basketball Rivalry. New York, NY: HarperCollins, 2006. Print.

Bryant, Howard. "Magic, Bird Were More than Rivals." ESPN.com. ESPN, 11 Mar. 2010. Web.

Carreon, Felix. "Women's Swimming and Diving Outlasts Buckeyes in Dual Meet." The Michigan Daily. N.p., 25 Jan. 2009. Web.

Castro, Janice. "LEON BING: In The Brutal World of L.A.'s Toughest Gangs." TIME 16 Mar. 1992: n. pag. Web.

Cochrane, Alan. "Celtic v Rangers: Alex Salmond Orders Summit to Tame Football Rivals." Www.telegraph.co.uk. The Telegraph, 4 Mar. 2011. Web.

Conner, Floyd. Football's Most Wanted: The Top 10 Book of the Great Game's Outrageous Characters, Fortunate Fumbles, and Other Oddities. Washington, D.C.: Brassey's, 2000. Print.

D'Amato, Gary, and Cliff Christl. Mudbaths & Bloodbaths: The inside Story of the Bears-Packers Rivalry. Black Earth, WI: Prairie Oak, 2005. Print.

Foer, Franklin. "How Soccer Explains the Pornography of Sects." How Soccer Explains the World: An Unlikely Theory of Globalization. New York: HarperCollins, 2004. 35-64. Print.

"Hokes Bluff Fire Probe Continuets." Gadsden Times 14 Sept. 1973: n. pag. Print.

Hoover, John E. "The Schooner Game." Oklahoma Latest & Breaking News, Sports, Weather, Entertainment, Business, Jobs, Homes, Cars, and Classified Ads OK. N.p., 9 June 2006. Web.

Johnston, Nick. "Glencoe, Hokes Bluff Renew Annual Rivalry Game Tonight." GadsdenTimes.com. N.p., 30 Oct. 2008. Web.

Karp, Hannah. "The Great Hipster Showdown." WSJ.com. Wall Street Journal, 13 May 2011. Web

Klosterman, Chuck. "8 33." Sex, Drugs, and Cocoa Puffs: A Low Culture Manifesto. New York: Scribner, 2004. 97-107. Print.

Klosterman, Chuck. Eating the Dinosaur. New York: Scribner, 2009. Print.

Merriam-Webster's Collegiate Dictionary -eleventh Ed.-. Springfield, MA: Merriam-Webster, Incorporated, 2003. Print.

Merron, Jeff. "Ohio State/Michigan vs. Army/Navy." ESPN.com Page 2. ESPN, n.d. Web.

Moore, Terence. "Why We Hate Duke." CNN. Cable News Network, 18 Mar. 2011. Web.

Nicar, Jim. "The Truth About Bevo - Traditions - UT History Central." The Truth About Bevo - Traditions - UT History Central. N.p., n.d. Web.

Park, Alice. "Football Fan Rage: How Home Team Losses Contribute to Domestic Violence | Healthland | TIME.com." Time. Time, 22 Mar. 2011. Web.

Phillips, Brian. "Celtic vs. Rangers, and What Happens When a Sports Rivalry Gets Completely out of Hand." Slate Magazine. N.p., 23 Mar. 2011. Web.

Steves, Rick. Rick Steves' Great Britain 2010. Berkeley, CA: Avalon Travel, 2009. Print.

"School Fire Investigated." Gadsden Times 13 Sept. 1973: n. pag. Print.

Simmons, Bill. "Strange Days Indeed." ESPN.com Page 2. N.p., Sept. 2001. Web.

Simmons, Bill. "Rolling a Seven." ESPN.com Page 2. N.p., Nov. 2001. Web.

Simmons, Bill. "The B.S. Report 6/17/2011 Part 1." Interview. Audio blog post. N.p., 17

"Texas 28, Oklahoma 2." Austin American-Statesman 1900: n. pag. Print.

Tipton, Jerry. "Kentucky.com." Revisiting the Roots of the UK-U of L Rivalry. Lexington Herald-Leader, 1 Jan. 2010. Web.

Wahl, Grant. "A Pacific Passion Play." ESPN.com. N.p., 23 May 2011. Web.

Ward, Doug. "Turf War in The heartland." ESPN. N.p., 02 July 2009. Web.

Winer, Matt. "The Worst Sports Fans in America." GQ. N.p., Apr. 2011. Web